Beyond Industrial Dualism

Conservation of Human Resources
Studies in the New Economy

Beyond Industrial Dualism: Market and Job Segmentation in the New Economy, Thierry J. Noyelle

Immigrant and Native Workers: Contrasts and Competition, Thomas R. Bailey

Computerization and the Transformation of Employment: Government, Hospitals, and Universities, Thomas M. Stanback, Jr.

Technology and Employment: Concepts and Clarification, Eli Ginzberg, Thierry J. Noyelle, and Thomas M. Stanback, Jr.

Beyond Industrial Dualism

Market and Job Segmentation in the New Economy

Thierry J. Noyelle

WESTVIEW PRESS

BOULDER AND LONDON

Conservation of Human Resources Studies in the New Economy

The material presented in this publication was prepared with financial assistance from the Rockefeller Foundation and the Ford Foundation. Points of view and opinions expressed in this book are solely those of the author and do not represent the positions or policies of either of these foundations.

Published in 1987 in the United States of America by Westview Press, Inc.; Frederick A. Praeger, Publisher; 5500 Central Avenue, Boulder, Colorado 80301

Library of Congress Cataloging-in-Publication Data
Noyelle, Thierry J.
  Beyond industrial dualism.
  (Conservation of Human Resources studies in the
new economy)
  Bibliography: p.
  Includes index.
  1. Market segmentation—Case studies. 2. Service
industries—United States—Case studies. 3. Service
industries workers—United States—Case studies.
4. Labor supply—United States—Case studies.
I. Title. II. Title: Job segmentation. III. Series.
HF5415.127.N69 1987   658.8'02   86-19068
ISBN 0-8133-7301-8

Composition for this book was provided by conversion of the author's computer tapes or word-processor disks.

Printed and bound in the United States of America

∞   The paper used in this publication meets the requirements of the American National Standard for Permanence of Paper for Printed Library Materials Z39.48-1984.

6   5   4   3   2   1

To Eileen

Contents

Tables and Figures

Tables

Figures

Foreword

In this important book, Dr. Thierry J. Noyelle presents new material and develops insightful analyses of a subject that many people hold strong opinions about—the changes that are taking place in the labor market. These far-reaching changes are the result of major structural developments, including the shift from manufacturing to services, the increasing internationalization of the world economy, the introduction of the new computer-communications technology, and other powerful factors.

Dr. Noyelle has contributed much to recent research on the shift of the economy to services and the restructuring of the urban system. In this book, he draws on his previous investigations to look more closely at the impact these forces are having on employment patterns in three major service industries: retailing, utilities, and finance.

It is always difficult to study and assess new trends before they become fully established; yet, that is one of the major tasks of researchers, conceptualizers, and policy-oriented analysts. It is dangerous to work with old paradigms when new trends have taken over. But the challenge remains: How are the new forces to be captured and assessed while they are still emergent?

The only answer seems to be for researchers to take selective forays into the new reality by studying institutions in the process of change. But economists usually avoid field research because it is costly in terms of time and energy; the investigator is aware that under even the best of circumstances one can have no way of knowing whether the findings are representative. In addition, economists are generally concerned with basic rather than emerging trends and tendencies and have little interest in aberrant cases.

In facing the challenge, Dr. Noyelle has found that the economist can benefit from field investigations if they are designed well and carried out effectively and if the researcher has a "feel" for the new, is able to elicit the cooperation of key institutions, and exercises restraint in generalizing his or her findings. Dr. Noyelle's good judgment in all of these respects has resulted in a rich yield. To illustrate at the risk of oversimplification, he found that the combined influences of heightened competition, new product development, and new technology led each of three prototypical large service corporations to engage in a major restructuring of their operations during the past two decades. This restructuring had the most profound impact on the personnel systems of the case study corporations. The internal labor markets that dominated the large manufacturing and service companies in the post–World War II era are undergoing a radical transformation. The classic mode for career mobility, whereby workers start at the bottom, learn by doing, and move up into high-level positions, is no longer feasible. Opportunities in the labor market are now determined by a multiplication of entry points for employees with different levels of education.

Dr. Noyelle emphasizes that despite this major transformation in patterns of career progression, it is incorrect to assume that the U.S. economy is characterized by a broad deskilling. In fact, upskilling is the trend. In addition, Dr. Noyelle explains how the weakening of internal labor markets, upskilling, and other organizational and personnel changes affect differently major groups of workers—white men and white women, minority men and minority women, and youth.

Dr. Noyelle provides the interested reader with a wealth of firsthand information about internal labor market changes that are under way in the new service economy as established employment patterns are being altered. He links his findings to preexisting theories and public policies and suggests the changes that must be contemplated if U.S. society is to respond to the new. For one book to do all this is no small contribution.

Eli Ginzberg
Director
Conservation of Human Resources
Columbia University

1

Introduction

We stand at a critical juncture in U.S. economic, social, and technological history. We are witnessing no less than the demise of an earlier economic system, centered on the mass production and mass marketing of industrial goods, and the emergence of a new paradigm of economic development emphasizing services, flexible production, and customized consumption (Stanback et al., 1981; Piore and Sabel, 1984; Ginzberg et al., 1986).

In the new paradigm, earlier ways of working, based on blue-collar factory employment, are being replaced by new ones, involving primarily white-collar office employment. Yesterday's highly standardized outputs churned out by high-volume assembly lines are giving place to today's heavily customized goods and services, increasingly produced in batch form or in smaller settings. Markets that were once mostly regional or national in scope are becoming increasingly international. The earlier strategic role of commodities, such as oil, electricity, steel, and chemicals, is being superseded by that of knowledge-based and information-based services, which are rapidly becoming the most critical inputs in economic processes. The latter transformation is best demonstrated by the formidable growth of producer services in the U.S. economy in recent years, both in employment and in value-added terms (Stanback et al., 1981).

Beyond Industrial Dualism

The rise of this new economy is bringing about a fundamental restructuring of both markets and jobs. Industrial dualism—the old way of structuring markets and jobs in the economy—is fast disappearing.

During the industrial period, spanning from the 1920s to the 1960s, there had emerged a structural dichotomy between a core economy comprising mostly large manufacturers and a peripheral economy dominated by small manufacturing firms and service organizations. Through-

1

out the core economy, large manufacturers tended to operate in an oligopolistic environment, where profits and employment were sheltered from the worst possible impacts of the business cycle. By comparison, firms in the peripheral economy faced a far more volatile, competitive environment. They typically bore the brunt of the impact of the business cycle (Averitt, 1968). Out of this market-based dichotomy, a particular structure of labor market segmentation had arisen. *Ceteris paribus*, workers employed by large employers from the core economy, faced far better prospects for long-term improvement in earnings and job mobility than those hired by firms from the peripheral economy (Doeringer and Piore, 1971).

In the late 1960s and early 1970s, as employment and output growth shifted to services and high-technology areas, a new market structure began taking shape. As a result of the trend toward deregulation and as a consequence of the rapid internationalization of the U.S. economy, the oligopolistic environment of many core sectors of the economy started crumbling. Many large firms began facing a marketplace far more competitive than that which they had known for the previous thirty or forty years. In turn, as the traditional differences between large, oligopolistic enterprises and small, competitive firms weakened and as the old distinction between "leading" manufacturing sectors and "lead" service sectors lessened, new differences arose between "declining" and "rising" firms. The meaning of "decline" or "rise" came to be associated with the capacity of firms, both small and large, whether service or manufacturing, to compete in an often less and less regulated and more and more internationalized marketplace. Not surprisingly, as had happened earlier, this transformation in the structuring of economic markets helped set in motion a major restructuring of labor markets. Aided by the steadily increasing flow of high school and college educated workers, and helped by the advent of new technologies, firms began emphasizing different uses of capital and labor, stressing quality of the labor force over sheer numbers. This new emphasis was in contrast to the previous period during which the principal concern of large corporations often had been to secure access to large labor pools to staff assembly lines and clerical operations.

The new emphasis on high-skilled work and well-trained labor is partly responsible for the recent decline in the role of the internal labor market and the increasing reliance of firms on the external labor market. The term "internal labor market" refers to the set of institutional mechanisms that large firms in the past had put in place, in house, to help train, prepare, and promote their own labor force as a way to continuously meet staffing needs. In place of internal labor markets, firms now operate with a multiplication of entry points, with levels of educational achievement (less than high school, high school, junior college, four-year college, professional schools) largely determining the job opportunities open to new employees. In turn, such changes are fueling the trend toward the widespread development of professions and paraprofessions. Newer, mostly laterally and occupationally-driven forms of mobility are now emphasized over the mostly vertical and firm-driven mobility formerly stressed in the internal labor markets.

This book attempts to identify some principal dimensions of this process of market and job restructuring by means of case studies of service companies. Special emphasis is placed on the job restructuring issue and, in particular, on the decline of internal labor markets. The book is the product of a research effort begun in 1982 under funding from the Rockefeller Foundation (Noyelle, 1983) and completed in 1985 with support from the Ford Foundation. While the materials presented here are primarily empirical, I do make a deliberate effort to extend beyond the case studies themselves and to conceptualize some of the trends that they indicate. This effort is tentative, not definitive. More will have to be known about the contours of the emerging service economy before a fully rounded conceptualization can be developed. In a sense, we are at a too early stage in the development of this new economy to understand fully the directions it is taking.

Outline of the Book

In the next chapter (Chapter 2), I point to processes of market and job segmentation that arose under industrial dualism and are now weakening or disappearing. The following three chapters illustrate empirically the changes hypothesized in Chapter 2 and identify emerging new processes of segmentation by means of three case studies of service firms. The case studies include a large retailing organization (Chapter 3), a large utility company (Chapter 4), and a large financial firm (Chapter 5). In Chapter 6, some attempts are made to conceptualize the new processes of segmentation and to show the new labor market interactions being brought about among major groups of workers. Critical issues such as skills, technology, education, training, and occupational mobility are examined. Chapter 7 concludes the book with policy pointers. This final chapter places special emphasis on some of the implications of my findings for employment opportunities for disadvantaged workers.

Before moving on to the next chapter, some words are needed to explain the choice of the three case study companies.

The three companies were selected because they are service firms, and because a central premise of this book is that the United States is moving toward an economy dominated by service organizations. Such a choice is helpful not only in shedding new light on the probable future but also in clarifying the past. Traditionally labor market economists have tended to be vague in their treatment of service firms, preferring to focus on manufacturing. The three case studies presented here demonstrate unambiguously that, in the past, large service firms were typically organized along the same working principles as their sister manufacturing organizations, making extensive use of internal labor market structures. The case studies also demonstrate that it is precisely the use of internal labor markets that is changing so dramatically.

The three firms were chosen to cover broad sectors of the economy: retailing, utility, and financial industries. To be sure, a more extensive study would have attempted to sample also the public, nonprofit (education and health), and manufacturing sectors. I have little doubt, however, that the transformations observed in these other sectors would mostly confirm the changes uncovered in the three sectors analyzed here. My colleague Thomas Stanback's ongoing work on technological change in the nonprofit and public sectors brings considerable support to the argument (Stanback, 1987).

The reader might wonder how general the findings can be when based on only three very large firms. It is important to understand that all three organizations are typical of what others are doing in their sector. R. H. Macy & Co., the retail organization selected for study, is, by all accounts, a trendsetter in human resource management in the industry. Interviews with other large retailers, such as J. C. Penney and Sears, confirm that. The insurance firm studied in Chapter 5 is prototypical of most others in its industry. This is confirmed by additional research which I have been conducting in the industry and which will be reported in a forthcoming book (Noyelle, forthcoming). The same can be said of New York Telephone whose experience is similar to that of many other utilities. In addition, as I will suggest in Chapter 6, the size of a firm as a determinant of the personnel organization appears far less important than it once was, thus weakening limitations arising from size-of-firm differences.

A major part of the three case studies is focused on identifying the structural characteristics that best define the quality of jobs. These characteristics include skills attached to jobs, the extent of on-the-job training, barriers to entry (prior skills, schooling, sex, race, or other), in-house opportunities for promotion, the short- and long-term stability of employment, and earnings.

The multidimensional nature of employment attributes has always made it difficult to develop broad measures of employment quality. Traditionally the notion of employment quality has been associated with the notion of opportunities for upward mobility. As suggested in the next chapter, under industrial dualism such opportunities tended to be found overwhelmingly in firms from the core sectors of the economy. In addition, employment attributes—income, skills, tenure provisions, training opportunities—tended to improve in conjunction with one another. In short, under industrial dualism the relationship between upward mobility and employment quality was typically straightforward.

This, however, might no longer be the case. If, as I believe, we have entered an era in which the role of internal labor markets has weakened and mobility is increasingly achieved through the external labor market, then the nature of the relationships between various employment attributes might also be changing. This major issue is addressed in Chapters 6 and 7, but is one that can hardly be assessed until the case studies have been reviewed. For this reason, the bulk of my effort in the three case study chapters focuses on assessing job characteristics one by one rather than on developing an interpretative model.

The three case studies are not written in exactly the same way. As I developed the material for the book, it became clear that each firm had something special to contribute to the understanding of the processes by which internal labor markets are being dismantled. At R. H. Macy & Co., it was the impact of the transformation of the managerial structure on the entire personnel system; at New York Telephone, the impact of changing skills, the need for aggressive affirmative action policies, and the new competition; at the insurance company, the impact of changing skills.

A final word about the case studies: These cases are meant to illustrate broad trends rather than emphasize findings highly specific to each firm. Nevertheless, at some point, changes cannot be divorced from the firm's particular history. This explains why each case is preceded by a short statement placing the firm in context; for that reason, the insurance firm preferred to remain anonymous. This forced me to be somewhat aloof in writing that particular case study. The other two firms were indifferent to identification.

The case material presented was developed through extensive interviews with key executives of the firms, industry analysts, union officials where appropriate as well as through research of public and corporate records.

In concluding this introduction, I wish to thank all of those who contributed to the preparation of this book. While the final responsibility for this manuscript is mine, many are those who helped to make it into a better book. First, I want to thank Eileen Appelbaum, Tom Bailey, Olivier Bertrand, Eli Ginzberg, Harvey Goldstein, Heidi Hartman, Larry Hirschhorn, Michael Piore, and Tom Stanback for their comments and criticisms on earlier versions of this manuscript. Second, I want to thank

Ellen Levine and Shoshana Vasheetz for their assistance in preparing the various drafts as well as Penny Peace for her editorial work. Last, but not least, I wish to thank the many individuals who agreed to be interviewed for this study. While most of my informers wanted to remain anonymous, each and every one of them has my deepest gratitude for her or his personal contribution.

2

The Rise of the New Economy and the Dismantling of Internal Labor Markets

To be sure, the advent of the new economy did not take place overnight. As always in the case of profound economic changes, the shift to the new era of services and computerized information technologies gained momentum over a period of several decades.

Nevertheless, the 1970s represent a critical turning point. Because the rise of the new economy involves the shift of capital and labor out of the smokestack industries and into the high-tech and service industries, the formidable acceleration of the internationalization of the economy during the 1970s—partly as a response to the two oil shocks of the decade—contributed greatly to speeding the redeployment of resources. Many older industries, once largely protected from foreign competition, were suddenly put to the wrenching test of worldwide competition and forced to adjust.

In addition, the new generation of information technologies introduced during the 1970s, including distributed data processing and early computer networking, helped to further this economic transformation. By now these technologies have been embedded in many new products and services; they have become central to the new processes of production and new ways of working; and they have challenged the corporation, which often must restructure and reorganize if it is to make productive use of these new technologies.

The Development of Information Technologies and the Rise of the Service Economy

The introduction of the first commercial computers in the mid-1950s marked the beginning of early modern computer-based information technologies. These computers helped put in place large automated

7

number-crunching capacity to assist corporations in performing many calculations at great speed and low unit cost. Mainframe computers were the principal pieces of machinery involved in this phase of automation

The era of computer-based information technologies brought major productivity increases in some sectors. In brokerage, transportation, and utility firms, for example, the new capability for data processing was the only way in which the vastly enlarged burdens of the "back office" could be handled after the early 1960s when the volume of transactions increased spectacularly.

In labor terms, mainframe technology generated a relatively well-defined demand for specialized personnel, primarily systems analysts, programmers, computer operators, and keypunchers. Its indirect labor impact on final users remained limited, however, since the use of the equipment was mediated by the systems divisions of large companies which employed much of the new, specialized personnel or by the mainframe data processing service bureaus which performed roughly the same function for a great number of middle- and small-sized companies.

In the late 1960s and early 1970s, a new era of computerization was launched following the introduction of freestanding minicomputer systems (later microcomputer systems), and on-line distributed data processing systems. This new era was made possible in part by the introduction of related technologies permitting massive data storage, high-speed processing capability (the microprocessor), and the development of user-friendly software.

In labor terms, distributed data processing began blurring the earlier distinction between computer specialists and users as computerized processing was gradually turned over to final users. This is the technology associated with the recent transformation of work and staffing in factories, back offices, engineering offices, sales offices, and the corporate offices of many manufacturing and service corporations. Distributed data processing is very much in evidence in the three case study companies presented in this book, be it in the form of electronic switching technology in the telephone industry, computerized cash register technology linked to accounting and inventory systems in retailing, or back-office processing systems in the financial sector.

While we are still very much in the midst of the introduction of distributed data processing systems, we already have begun moving into the next era of information technologies. Networking and telecommunications technologies are at the core of the new phase of information technologies. Computerized systems which today remain mostly freestanding at the office, shop, or department level are increasingly being linked with one another so that extensive computerized interactions can occur among a firm's departments, consumers and firms, and suppliers and customers. As this new era progresses, the three basic modes of communications—voice, data, and, later, image—are going to be increasingly brought together to permit merged uses. In labor terms, its impact is likely to be mostly indirect and widely diffused as productivity increases ripple far and deep throughout the economy and as consumers, workers, and firms alter their ways of relating to each other.

The cumulative labor impact of these information technologies is analyzed in some detail in the three case studies. Still, one must remain mindful not to unduly overplay the role of new technologies. On the basis of the case studies, it can also be argued that the introduction of information technologies often does no more than simply facilitate or accelerate transformations of labor and employment processes already under way.

For that very reason, it is also useful to point to the sheer magnitude of the impact of the recent shift to the services on the industrial occupational structure of the new economy. Between 1970 and the last quarter of 1984, 27.2 million net new jobs (U.S. Department of Labor, *Employment and Earnings*, various issues) were added to the economy, of which nearly 95 percent were in the service industries. Looking only at the 1980s, the shift to the services was even sharper. By late 1984, when employment in the goods-producing industries—agriculture, mining, construction, and manufacturing—reached a new cyclical peak, their level had not even caught up with that of the previous 1980 peak. In net terms, this meant that employment growth since early 1981 had been 100 percent in the service industries.

Translated into occupational terms, the service transformation of the labor market means that today more than seven out of every ten workers are now employed in either white-collar or service occupations. This is the result of the cumulative impact of (1) the sharp drop in the share of blue-collar workers between 1965 and 1983, from 39.2 percent to 29.3 percent of the nonagricultural labor force (U.S. Department of Labor, *Employment and Earnings*, various issues); (2) the shift in growth to service industries dominated by white-collar or service-worker occupations; and (3) technological changes in manufacturing, accelerating the shift to managerial, engineering, technical, sales, or clerical occupations within the traditionally blue-collar dominated sectors.

In broad terms, these shifts have been tilted toward women and minority workers. During the same 1970–1984 period, nearly two-thirds of the new jobs have been filled by members of these groups. As a result, by late 1984 white males no longer constituted the majority of

the labor force. From nearly 55 percent in 1970, their share had dropped
to 49.5 percent by late 1984.

Industrial Dual Labor Markets

Job Segmentation

To identify emerging labor markets, it is useful to understand those
markets out of which they are being restructured. One line of argument
developed during the 1960s and 1970s to explain industrial labor markets
was the theory of dual labor markets. Although often criticized for
lacking intellectual rigor, the theory provided many an implicit conceptual
underpinning to employment policies developed under the impulse of
the Great Society programs. While the emphasis on labor market segmentation developed in the 1960s and 1970s by the proponents of dual
labor market theory was not new—having attracted attention as early
as the 1930s and 1940s—it did spur a large output of empirical and
conceptual literature from a new generation of economists, ranging, for
example, from Doeringer and Piore (1971) to Gordon, Edwards, and
Reich (1982).

In its simplest formulation, the theory held that the market dichotomy
between the core and the peripheral economy was itself at the root of
a labor market dichotomy between primary and secondary job segments.
With additional refinements, including separating the primary segment
into two subsegments, the theory typically identified three major groups
of jobs:

1. *Independent primary jobs:* Technical, professional, managerial, and
   craft jobs; requiring some general skills and problem-solving abil-
   ities; high pay with some job security; rewards to personal characteristics of initiative and general analytic ability. Technical and
   professional jobs fed by labor markets beginning with the formal
   education screening process and then reproduced through screening
   process based both on credentials and work experience. Craft jobs
   still fed through apprenticeship systems.
2. *Subordinate primary jobs:* Decent pay and substantial job security;
   low general skill requirements; some skills learned on the job
   through experience; authority relations and internal job structures
   very important fulcrum for corporate administration of production
   process and individual's personal advancement. Workers get such
   jobs through personal contacts as much as through formal labor
   market processes, and advancement comes much more easily

through internal promotion than job-hopping in the external labor market.

3. *Secondary jobs:* In small firms or small shops/offices of large firms; low pay; few skills required; no opportunity for advancement; virtually no inducements for workers to remain on the job. Jobs filled through casual and virtually random general labor market shape-ups and advertisement. (Employment offices also feed workers into these jobs.) (Gordon, 1979, pp. 36–37).

In general, each segment was seen as offering widely different opportunities in pay, skills, work autonomy, or mobility prospect, ranging from very good in the highest segment to very poor in the lowest. Hence, while workers might have entered the labor market at the start of their careers with roughly similar individual endowments in human capital, they would end in sharply different positions based simply on the segment which they entered originally. These and other characteristics were identified in empirical studies by Osterman, Buchelle, Carnoy, and Rumberger, and many others and have been summarized by Edwards (1979, especially Chapter 9) and Paul Ryan (Wilkinson, 1981).

Intricately woven within this job segmentation, based on market structure, was another level of segmentation, based on sexism and racism. Segmentation theorists argued that overt sexism and racism had been used to close off employment to women and minority workers in the independent primary segment. Most women and minorities were channeled into secondary jobs, or into subordinate primary jobs with very restricted mobility opportunities (Edwards, Reich, and Gordon, 1973, introductory chapter).

Internal Labor Markets

A critical element in the dynamics of segmentation was the existence of internal labor market structures in primary-sector firms and, conversely, the usual lack of equivalent structures in secondary-sector firms. As mentioned in the previous chapter, internal labor markets played a major role in preparing and moving about workers to staff the many echelons of corporate organizations. A central premise of this book is that understanding the extent to which the role of internal labor markets has weakened in recent years provides critical clues in identifying the current transformation of job segmentation.

The reliance of many firms on internal labor markets has been illustrated extensively. But the tendency, in the past, has been to assume that these structures were found mostly in the very large manufacturing firms which typified the industrial era. The case studies presented in the next three chapters suggest that many large service firms also made use of them. This, in itself, is an important finding. It says that the recent departure from a widespread reliance on internal labor markets cannot simply be ascribed to the decline of manufacturing firms and the rise of service firms, but instead must be seen as part of a total labor market transformation affecting both manufacturing and service industries.

As I show in the next three chapters, most workers in the insurance industry used to enter the job ladder at the very bottom straight out of high school, starting as messengers or file clerks. Through on-the-job training and seniority, they would move up the ranks. Over the years, many could expect to make their way up to technical, professional, or managerial positions, having progressed from messenger to clerk, claim examiner, policy rater, and later to assistant underwriter or underwriter. In department stores, workers would enter as stockroom clerks and move on to sales positions, possibly to a commissioned sales position in a high-ticket department (furniture, household, appliances, etc.). After some years of experience, a number of them would progress further to department manager, assistant buyer, and buyer positions. Similar examples could be found in banks, utilities, and many other service organizations. To repeat, sexism and racism, however, were often used to create sex- or race-labeled occupations, restricting the bulk of mobility opportunities available through internal labor markets to white males while channeling women and minority workers into dead-end jobs. In many respects, however, these earlier models of labor market dynamics have been overtaken by sweeping historical changes.

The 1970s: A Period of Transition

A close examination of labor market transformation during the 1970s points to major changes, including a fundamental weakening of internal job ladders. Where did changes come from? They originated from several forces, including the rise in the share of women and minority workers in the labor force, the enforcement of Equal Employment Opportunity (EEO), the increased importance of higher education, and the introduction of new technologies into the workplace.

The Rise of Women and Minority Workers and the Advent of Equal Employment Opportunity

In an informal way, the first major challenge to the integrity of the white-male-dominated internal labor market structures came from the sheer growing weight of female and minority workers in the economy.

At some point, closing off certain employment opportunities to those workers became dysfunctional simply because it arbitrarily restricted the size of the labor pool available to employers and constrained growth. In Chapter 4, I take note of such an artificial shortage with the example of craft positions at New York Telephone arbitrarily closed off to women and minority workers until the early 1970s.

In a structural way, the challenge to the integrity of white-male-dominated internal labor markets came with the advent of EEO following the Civil Rights Act of 1964. Still, the full strength of EEO was slow to set in motion. For a number of years, the U.S. EEO Commission (EEO-C) searched for a strategy that would yield greater institutional impact than the practice of case-by-case litigation of discrimination complaints which it pursued at first. The answer came in January 1973 when the American Telephone & Telegraph Company (the "old" AT&T), the EEO-C, the U.S. Department of Justice, and the U.S. Department of Labor agreed to a consent decree that became a milestone in EEO-C enforcement. Not only was AT&T then the largest private sector employer, with nearly one million employees, but between 1965 and 1970 over 2,000 individual cases had been filed with EEO-C charging AT&T with employment discrimination—a startling near 10 percent of all cases filed with the agency (Northrup and Larson, 1979).

The AT&T-EEO consent decree represented the first time that EEO-C stepped away from the nearly impossible task of case-by-case litigation. The message to other employers was meant to be, at the time at least, unequivocal: Discrimination in the workplace was illegal, and EEO objectives would be enforced vigorously. In addition, the decree was the first major instance in which financial compensation was sought to redress discrimination suffered by whole classes of workers. The decree established detailed employment goals and targets as well as new hiring and internal promotion procedures at AT&T. Over time, these practices were all meant to help the company eliminate the impact of its earlier discriminatory practices vis-à-vis female and minority workers.

A year later (April 1974), buoyed by its settlement with AT&T, EEO-C claimed another major milestone by getting nine major firms in the steel industry to agree to a major consent decree (Ichniowski, 1983). As in the case of the AT&T-EEO decree, the importance of the steel decree lay in part in the sheer number of workers affected since nearly three-quarters of a million workers were then employed by the industry. In contrast to the AT&T-EEO-C settlement, however, union involvement was sought throughout the negotiation of this new decree. In so doing, some of the very troublesome litigation that ensued following the AT&T-EEO decree was avoided.

The two decrees, and others developed during the years that followed, had a number of points in common. Most dealt with industries belonging to the primary segment of the economy, dominated by a few large or very large employers on the demand side and, typically, a few powerful unions on the supply side. In short, most dealt with industries in which the discriminating institutions on both the demand and the supply sides of the labor market were easily identifiable and targetable.

Furthermore, these decrees involved industries with firms characterized by strong internal mobility ladders. In these industries, the usual process of discrimination involved confining the entry of women and minority workers into industrial departments characterized by short ladders and limited upward-mobility opportunities and forbidding crossover from less favorable to more favorable departments. Typically, there had been some complicity on the part of white-male-dominated unions preserving the status quo.

Each of these decrees attempted to eliminate discrimination by striking at the very core of these arrangements in a similar manner: (1) by extending seniority rights—typically limited to departmental seniority— to the entire company in order to facilitate lateral moves of women and minorities into better departments; (2) by establishing objectives for increasing the number of women and minority workers in particular occupational ranks. These objectives were to be achieved over a limited time period even if they required overriding the seniority rights of white male workers; and, finally, (3) by getting firms to invest additional, often very substantial, training money to prepare women and minority workers for the positions that were being opened to them. In other words, the central principle behind these decrees was to eliminate discrimination by extending the benefits of internal labor markets to women and minority workers.

Had everything else remained unchanged, the EEO challenge might have considerably weakened sex and race discrimination in the workplace. While major gains were achieved as a direct result of some of these decrees (as I show in several places in this book), at times the gains were not as extensive as had been hoped. This is partly because at the same time that EEO policies were gaining speed, other forces came into play that began to weaken the role of internal labor markets across a broad range of industries. Hence, a basic dimension of EEO strategy— aggressive internal promotion of women and minority workers—was undermined. Some women and minority workers continued to advance to higher echelons, but their progress became increasingly dependent on a different set of factors, involving educational credentials and the conditions under which they were acquired. Hence, while overt sex and race discrimination in the workplace might have been weakened, indirect and hidden forms of discrimination might have crept back in via the determinants of hiring. This fundamental change is elaborated in the case study chapters and in Chapter 6.

The Dismantling of Internal Labor Markets

The second and most serious challenge to the integrity of industrial dual labor markets came from the dismantling of various elements critical to the articulation of internal labor markets.

Increasingly firms came under pressure to externalize training costs and responsibilities, to rely more extensively than they had earlier on the external labor markets for staffing, and to rearrange accordingly the way they hired and promoted people. Two primary forces were responsible for driving this new dynamic: the steady expansion of schooling and higher education throughout the postwar decades and the advent of distributed data processing technologies.

The Postwar Expansion of Schooling and Higher Education and Its Impact on Hiring Requirements. The first cause of change stemmed from the postwar expansion of schooling and the higher educational system. It became largely a case of supply changes leading to demand changes. By changing so radically the makeup of the labor supply, the expansion of the educational system put pressure on all firms to adjust their hiring procedures and to accommodate themselves to the availability of a labor supply increasingly differentiated by various grades and shades of education. For example, whereas only slightly more than 10 percent of those between ages 25 and 29 had received four years or more of college education in 1960, by 1980 this share had risen to nearly 25 percent of the same age population.

The expansion of formal education led to a major shift to outside hiring, first felt most strongly among administrative, professional, and managerial personnel—the so-called exempt workers. The result of this shift was the simultaneous weakening of those traditional internal ladders designed to move the best workers from nonexempt positions to supervisory and middle-managerial positions. In concrete terms, this meant that one could no longer expect to rise from the bottom to a buyer for a major retailing organization or an executive for a major insurance company.

Clearly, the early 1970s represented a turning point as the cumulative effect of several decades of expansion of the educational system and the coming of age of the baby boom generation were finally being felt massively on the supply side of the labor market. Yet some of these changes had been in the making for some time. In Chapter 3, for example, I date some of the changes in the retailing sector as far back as the mid-1960s.

The Impact of the New Technology on Skill Requirements and the Acceleration of Changes in Hiring and Mobility Opportunities. Whereas the changes in hiring and mobility opportunities had been mostly supply driven in the early and mid-1970s, changes in the late 1970s and early 1980s were both supply and demand driven. They were caused by two factors: (1) the introduction of distributed data processing technologies, which had a major impact on skills and (2) the response of firms to skill changes including gearing middle-level work increasingly toward workers with post–high school training and education.

Broadly speaking then, the era of distributed data processing technologies acted to reinforce the tendency toward a weakening of internal ladders. This occurred for several reasons, which are examined in more detail in Chapter 6, but which need to be outlined for the purpose of the present argument.

As the introduction of distributed data processing proceeded, a fundamental transformation and reorganization around the processing of information through interactions and computerized systems took hold. At first, the jobs most directly affected appear to have been those in the middle range of the occupational structure, ranging from relatively low-level clerical positions and blue-collar operative positions all the way to low-level and middle-level technical workers. Still, the transformation of high-level technical, professional, and managerial workers followed closely (Hirschhorn, 1984; Bertrand and Noyelle, 1984; Appelbaum, 1984). Only in the case of the lowest-level occupations—primarily laborers, service workers, and low-level sales and clerical workers—has it seemed that the new technology has had, thus far, very limited direct impact on work and skills.

To a very large extent, the process of work transformation did not lead to downskilling, as was first argued by many, but typically to some degree of upskilling, even though some downskilling might have occurred in some situations. Upskilling came about for two principal reasons: (1) because the most efficient use of the new technology often led to a reintegration of tasks once parceled out among many echelons of workers and (2) because as intelligent systems took over processing functions, workers were left with diagnostic and problem-solving functions (e.g., Appelbaum, 1984; Adler, 1984; others reviewed in Bertrand and Noyelle, 1984).

In addition to upskilling, the introduction of the new information technologies led toward a kind of universalization or homogenization of skills demanded across a wide range of industries, allowing for greater externalization of training for many middle-level workers. Many occupations have now become more generic and less firm specific than they once were. For example, the job of a bank clerk processing letters of credit or fund transfers on a computerized system or that of an insurance examiner processing claims has become not only more demanding in terms of skills but also increasingly similar in terms of needed skills: computer-oriented algorithmic logic has replaced many firm-specific idiosyncratic practices. This is true even though these jobs are found in industries widely differing in terms of the business each conducts. Economist Eileen Appelbaum points to the rapid development of temporary clerical help agencies in the late 1970s and early 1980s as a direct consequence of this increasing transferability of clerical skills across many business areas (Appelbaum, 1985). A direct result of this skill transformation has been a shift in the demand for training away from on-the-job training mechanisms within the firm to the vocational educational institutions, the community colleges, or even the four-year colleges. In turn, this shift has further undermined the raison d'être of the old internal labor market.

Technological Change and Increasing Institutional and Geographic Mobility. One might have expected that upskilling would indirectly strengthen the labor market position of increasingly larger groups of workers, leading to rising earnings and improved opportunities for occupational mobility. This has not necessarily been the case. The concomitant universalization of skills has often weakened the degree of labor market sheltering that was once associated with many industry-specific or firm-specific skills, especially in the context of weakening unionization. This is why "downwaging" appears to have occurred often along with "upskilling."

For example, the new technology makes increasingly feasible and cost efficient the geographic separation of back-office functions (dominated by clerical and service-worker occupations) from front-office functions (dominated by technical, sales, professional, or managerial occupations). This greater geographic mobility of the back office further contributes to breaking the institutional job linkages that used to exist when entire departments, from bottom up, were located in the same physical location. In addition, by opening the range of possible locations, it puts a broader number of workers in competition with one another. Finally, it puts new pressures on individual workers at a time when the rise in two-wage-earner households tends to hinder geographic mobility for a growing number of workers.

Conclusion

In concluding, the 1970s saw considerable turmoil affecting the ways in which employment opportunities had been structured during the earlier, industrial era. As noted at the outset of this book, the following three chapters supply evidence to support the hypothesis of the dismantling of internal labor markets and help in the discovery of new processes of segmentation.

TABLE 3.3
Percentage Sales of R. H. Macy & Co. in Downtown and Suburban Stores, 1957–1976

	6 Downtown Flagship Stores (%)	Suburban and Other Stores (%)	Total R. H. Macy & Co. (%)	Total Sales R. H. Macy & Co. ($ mill.)
1957	68.0	32.0	100.0	448
1966	39.0	61.0	100.0	719
1976	22.0	78.0	100.0	1,469

Source: R. H. Macy & Co., *Annual Reports,* 1966 and 1976; *Barron's,* Feb. 2, 1973.

The 1950s and 1960s:
R. H. Macy & Co.'s Weak Performance

Confronted with fierce competition, many chains attempted to retaliate by trying to behave like the discounters. Most never did well, however, because of sharp differences in cost structure. To a large extent, this was the strategy pursued by R. H. Macy & Co. during the late 1950s and the 1960s, a period during which the company became increasingly suburbanized. The share of sales from its suburban stores grew from 32 to 61 percent between 1957 and 1966 (see Table 3.3). Yet, it was largely unable to capitalize on the prosperity of the 1950s and early 1960s. Its profits were low throughout the 1950s and early 1960s, and it would take close to ten years (1965–1975) for the company to restore profits to levels comparable to those of the late 1940s (see Figure 3.1).

The 1970s: R. H. Macy & Co.'s Comeback

R. H. Macy & Co.'s comeback was first engineered at its Bamberger's division by Herbert Seegal and Edward S. Finkelstein, who later would play a major role in turning around the entire R. H. Macy & Co. organization (Ellis, 1978).

Unlike other Macy divisions, Bamberger's never attempted to compete head on with the discounters. Instead, it tried to preserve and promote an image of fashion and quality unmatched by the discounters. In retrospect, Seegal and Finkelstein's savvy was in foreseeing earlier than other merchandisers the rise of an upscale consumer class. This group would become critical to financial success during the late 1970s and early 1980s, a time when middle-income consumers would face increasing financial stress. As Ellis (1978) put it, "[Bamberger's] merchandising

FIGURE 3.1
Net Earnings to Net Worth Ratio of R. H. Macy & Co., 1945–1980

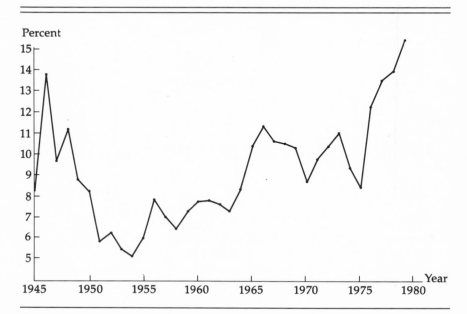

Source: Moody's Industrial Manuals (New York: Moody's Investors Service, several years).

efforts were geared to 'narrow and deep' assortments of wanted classifications appealing to specific customer types, with particular emphasis on the young adult market, the cutting edge of changing societal values, lifestyles, and fashion trends."

The success of the strategy was unmistakable. Throughout much of the 1960s and early 1970s, Bamberger's profits carried R. H. Macy & Co. (see Table 3.4). With such a strong record, Seegal went on to head the corporation in the early 1970s, and Finkelstein to manage Macy's California where new blood was needed. In just a few years, Finkelstein turned around Macy's California with a strategy similar to the one he and Seegal used at Bamberger's. By the mid–1970s, Finkelstein returned to the East Coast to take on a yet tougher assignment—Macy's New York. Later, he would replace Seegal when the latter retired as chief executive officer.

In New York Finkelstein placed greater emphasis on rebuilding the flagship store, which, because of its sheer size and because of Manhattan's comeback played a much greater role in carrying out the image of the

TABLE 3.4
R. H. Macy & Co.: Sales and Pretax Income by Operating Division, 1945–1981

	1945	1950	1960	1971	1975	1981
Retail Sales						
All Divisions ($ mill.)	197	321	509	957	1,298	2,657
All Divisions (%)	100.0	100.0	100.0	100.0	100.0	100.0
Macy's New York	61.6	57.2	na	43.3	35.8	31.4
Bamberger's	21.2	17.7	na	26.2	28.9	30.0
Macy's California	—	5.7	na	15.9	19.6	24.3
Davison-Paxon	10.2	9.6	na	5.9	6.9	7.1
Lasalle & Koch	7.0	5.9	na	3.0	2.5	7.2[a]
Macy's Missouri-Kansas	—	3.7	na	5.7	6.2	
Pretax Income						
All Divisions ($ mill.)	14	11	25	43	50	226
All Divisions (%)	100.0	100.0	100.0	100.0	100.0	100.0
Macy's New York	55.0	81.3	na	24.6	(25.8)[b]	24.3
Bamberger's	18.9	22.1	na	45.8	61.8	38.2
Macy's California	—	(0.7)	na	18.8	50.6	31.0
Davison-Paxon	14.6	8.3	na	6.8	4.7	7.3
Lasalle & Koch	11.6	5.9	na	0.7	1.4	(1.0)[c]
Macy's Missouri-Kansas	—	(16.9)	na	3.3	7.5	

na = not available.
( ) indicates a loss.

[a] Lasalle & Koch and Macy's Missouri-Kansas were merged in 1980 to form Macy's Midwest.
[b] Macy's New York lost money in 1974, 1975, and 1976.
[c] Macy's Midwest lost money in 1980, 1981, and 1982.

Source: R. H. Macy & Co., *Annual Reports*, 1945 and 1950; and Joseph Ellis, *R. H. Macy & Co.*, Research Report (New York: Goldman Sachs Investment, April 10, 1978).

division. Between 1975 and 1980, more than $20 million was spent to renovate Herald Square alone, bringing about first the renovation of the sixth floor (mostly domestics), then the opening of "The Cellar" (in 1976),[1] and later a major floor-by-floor refurbishing of the entire store (still in progress).

The results in the late 1970s were startling, both in the New York division and elsewhere in the organization. Profits rebounded back (see Figure 3.1 and Table 3.4). R. H. Macy & Co. was now "boasting a stylish new image," emphasizing the fashionable and the trendy, having succeeded in remaining family oriented while repositioning itself upscale (*Barron's*, 1978).

The Transformation of the Personnel Organization

The "Merchant Prince" System

In the years following World War II, the R. H. Macy & Co. organization remained centered on its flagship stores, with a very lean divisional and corporate structure. Like most other department stores at the time, Macy's was organized, as it always had been, as a group of "departments," with buyers running departments like small enterprises. Buyers were responsible for goods procurement (merchandising functions), promotion (marketing functions), sales, and staffing (personnel functions). They were responsible for promoting their own employees. They paid rent, light, and other fixed and variable costs on a prorated basis. They held regular meetings with their staff to learn which goods were selling, which were not, which needed reordering, and which needed to be discounted. In short, departments were true profit centers, with the "merchant princes" in command.

As the company began opening branches, a divisional staff to ensure coordination was needed. At first, however, the responsibilities of the corporate staff remained limited. Departments continued to operate as they always had except for one difference. Buyers were now also in charge of the clone departments in the branches, visiting them several times a week to take stock of needs and performance. But as the responsibilities of buyers expanded, their task became increasingly complex.

The sheer buildup in the number of branches made the job of the buyers increasingly difficult. The larger the number of branches, the more hectic the buyers' work schedule became as visits to branches multiplied. The growing importance of media advertising made it harder for buyers to handle marketing functions, especially in view of the growing need to promote an overall corporate image across departments and in several market areas at once. In addition, the buyers' responsibilities for personnel functions became rapidly unmanageable as new branches opened and as new shifts were added to staff the longer business hours. Last, buyers grew less and less attentive to the merchandising function itself because their time was appropriated by other responsibilities. This occurred at the very same time that merchandising increased in complexity, options multiplied, and product runs shortened.[2]

By all accounts, trailing productivity, high labor costs, and low profits during the 1950s and early 1960s were indicative of corporate organization that had become highly dysfunctional. A complete revamping of R. H. Macy & Co.'s entire personnel organization was being called for.

From Merchant Princes to Professional Managers:
The Introduction of the Orbit System

Bamberger's was the first division to break away from the old "merchant prince" system when in 1963 it introduced the *orbit system*. It was a radical attempt to reorganize Bamberger's entire supervisory and executive structure. It was the first such initiative in the industry, soon to be copied by other Macy divisions and even other retailers.

The orbit system split the old merchant prince system into several clearly defined functional lines, including merchandising, store management, sales promotion, personnel, financial audit, and operations and control, each with its own line of command and responsibilities. The fundamental innovation was, of course, in separating merchandising from store management responsibilities, traditionally the two main thrusts of the management effort. Merchandising was brought under the authority of divisional merchandise administrators who were placed in charge of managing the purchases made by buyers and assistant buyers at the divisional level. Store management was put under the full authority of store managers who oversaw merchandise managers (in charge of procurement), group managers (in charge of overseeing groups of departments), and department sales managers.

The separation between merchandising and store management introduced a more complex sharing of responsibilities for profits and losses than before, with buyers controlling merchandising expenses and store managers controlling selling expenses but with neither having control over both. The new system required instituting a complex back-and-forth reporting system between the merchandising line and the buying line and developing an acute understanding on both parts of what the other was doing. To promote understanding and cross-reporting, a new career-ladder structure was developed at Bamberger's, shifting executives back and forth from store management to merchandising. Called the orbit system, this structure was extended later to other divisions and has remained largely unchanged since it was first introduced.

Under the orbit system (see Figure 3.2), new managers are brought straight onto the executive ladder as department sales managers. Department managers work in stores on the sales floor; supervise sales clerks; keep an eye on stock; and keep in touch with assistant buyers and buyers. They make recommendations and have some training responsibilities for sales clerks under them. Their direct supervisor is the group manager (or area manager), also in the store line. Today, most of the department sales managers are new hires from college or transfers from other firms. While some divisions continue promoting a few of their best employees from nonexempt ranks to these junior executive

FIGURE 3.2
The Orbit System: Lines of Promotion and Lines of Reporting in Merchandising
and Store Operations

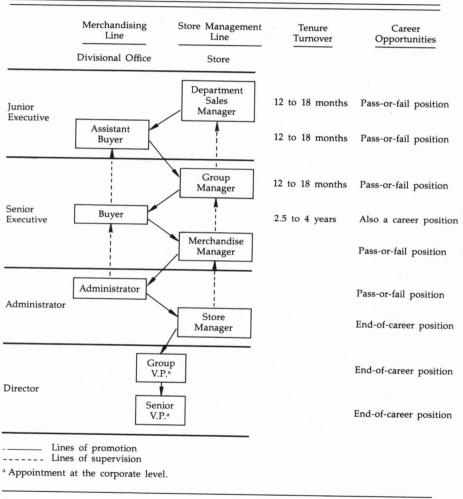

	Merchandising Line	Store Management Line	Tenure Turnover	Career Opportunities
	Divisional Office	Store		
Junior Executive	Assistant Buyer	Department Sales Manager	12 to 18 months	Pass-or-fail position
			12 to 18 months	Pass-or-fail position
Senior Executive	Buyer	Group Manager	12 to 18 months	Pass-or-fail position
		Merchandise Manager	2.5 to 4 years	Also a career position
				Pass-or-fail position
Administrator	Administrator	Store Manager		Pass-or-fail position
				End-of-career position
Director	Group V.P.[a]			End-of-career position
	Senior V.P.[a]			End-of-career position

————— Lines of promotion
- - - - - - Lines of supervision
[a] Appointment at the corporate level.

Source: R. H. Macy & Co., company documents.

positions, the practice has become exceptional. (I return to this issue later in the chapter.) Sales managers stay in the job from 12 to 18 months before being promoted to an assistant buyer position (or fired if performance is not satisfactory). The position of assistant buyer is pretty much what the title implies. It is also a "pass-or-fail" position and lasts from one year to 18 months.

From assistant buyer, the junior executive moves back into the store line as a group manager. Group managers supervise groups of sales managers in a particular functional area (for example, all of "domestics": sheets, towels, blankets, comforters, etc.). They are responsible for the training of sales managers and for the total dollar volume of sales in their area. The group manager position is again a pass-or-fail position, with a duration from one year to 18 months.

From the group manager level, the next step is to the position of buyer, again at the divisional level. Unlike previous promotions, this position often becomes a career position. There are even provisions for executives who have moved further up in the hierarchy to return to such a position if it seems best suited to their professional interest. For those who continue on, a minimum of 2–1/2 to 4 years is required as a buyer, which involves at least two assignments—one in low-volume and one in high-volume classifications.

The next position is back in the store line at the merchandise manager level, where the responsibility involves global procurement for a given store and the supervision of group managers and sales managers in small departments that do not receive direct supervision from group managers. This is shown graphically in Figure 3.3.

In the largest stores (flagship stores), there are usually three merchandise managers, respectively, for hard goods, soft goods, and The Cellar. From there on, the back-and-forth shifting process between the store and the divisional lines continues, first by a move to an administrator's position (involving the supervision of a group of buyers), then to a store manager position, followed by a group vice-president position (usually a regional administrator of stores), and so on to the highest echelons of the corporate ladder.

During the 1970s, with the growing importance of personnel, sales promotion, financial audit, and operations and control, similar attention was placed on developing extensive and formal ladder systems in these four areas. As with buying and store management, the notion of moving executives back and forth from the store to the division was institutionalized, although here mobility does not involve moving across functional lines. As an example, Figure 3.4 shows the structure of promotions for executives in the personnel area.

FIGURE 3.3
Responsibilities of Merchandise Managers and Group Managers Under the Orbit System

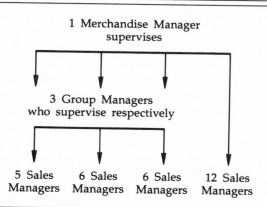

1 Merchandise Manager
supervises

3 Group Managers
who supervise respectively

| 5 Sales | 6 Sales | 6 Sales | 12 Sales |
| Managers | Managers | Managers | Managers |

Source: R. H. Macy & Co., company documents.

The result of the extensive layering of executive echelons introduced through the orbit system is shown in Table 3.5. Most junior executives are sales managers or assistant buyers, roughly in the ratio of 3 to 1. Among sales managers, the annual turnover is high, about 30 to 40 percent, due to both quits and moves to assistant buyer positions (each explaining about half of the turnover ratio). Most senior executives are buyers, and most administrators are store managers.

To conclude, the introduction of the orbit system had several major objectives:

1. To unbundle the two key functions—merchandising and sales—in order to make each more manageable than it was under the old merchant prince system.
2. To develop an organizational structure that would refocus on merchandising while maintaining proper attention to sales.
3. To introduce a system of promotions characterized by high turnover in the lowest executive echelons in order to avoid costly overloading of middle-management ranks (department sales manager and assistant buyers).

Staffing the Stores

Having broken the hold of buyers on departmental staff, the introduction of the orbit system made possible changes in the way stores

FIGURE 3.4
The Orbit System: Lines of Promotion in Personnel

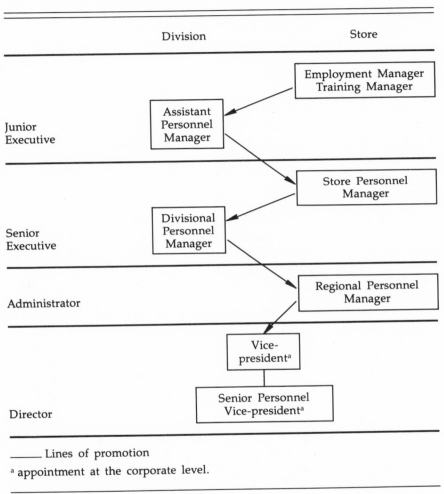

_____ Lines of promotion

[a] appointment at the corporate level.

Source: R. H. Macy & Co., company documents.

were being staffed and an aggressive response to labor cost competition from other, leaner retail organizations. The results were dramatic.

First, there was a rapid shift to part-time employment. In the mid-1960s, roughly 65 percent of nonexempt personnel was employed full-time and 35 percent part-time. By the late 1970s, these proportions had been reversed. In part, the growth in part-time employment was a result of the increase in open hours and the need for staffing less than full-

TABLE 3.5
Approximate Distribution of Bamberger's Executives, Early 1980s

Appointment Level	Number
Junior Executive	1,500
Senior Executive	500
Administrator	29
Director	13
Principal	2

Source: R. H. Macy & Co., company documents.

time shifts on evenings and weekends. However, it also reflected a move to a strategy emphasizing greater use of part-time personnel as a way to cap the growth in aggregate labor costs.

Second, there was a marked departure from an earlier emphasis on mobility opportunities from nonexempt to junior executive positions, a consequence of the creation of the new entry point for college graduates at the department manager level.

Third, the company experienced a marked shift in the composition of the nonexempt staff—once overwhelmingly dominated by mature, white females—towards youth and minorities.

Today, about 80 percent of the company's nonexempt staff works on the sales floor, with the remaining 20 percent in supporting areas (back offices, shipping and receiving docks, stockrooms, and distribution centers). Seventy percent of the sales staff is employed on a part-time basis and 30 percent on a full-time basis. In the supporting areas, the ratios are roughly reversed.

Twenty-five years ago, the business was mostly a nine-to-five operation. Sales areas were staffed with a full-time, nine-to-five shift and a 25-hour-a-week, part-time shift in the afternoon (usually from 11:00 A.M. to 4:30 P.M.) to help out in the period of heavier customer traffic. Part-time employees were mostly housewives who came to work after sending their children off to school and returned home early in the evening. In the view of one executive interviewed for this case study, these women went to work partly to supplement family income and partly to get away from the loneliness of their house (especially for those living in the suburbs). They tended to constitute a particularly reliable pool of workers and were often fairly well educated and highly motivated. In addition, they rarely demanded extensive involvement in the structure of promotions available to full-time workers, if only because they often did not seek extensive involvement in a work life.

Today, department stores have become seven-day, five-evening-a-week businesses (open roughly 65 hours a week). Stores are now staffed with three shifts of employees: "full timers" who work weekdays during the daytime (37–1/2 to 40 hours a week), "part timers" who work between the hours of 11:00 A.M. and 4:30 P.M. (20–25 hours a week), and "short-hour employees" who work weeknights and weekends.[3]

Most new hires come in at the base minimum hourly wage rate for the area and must go through a paid basic training program of 22 hours. The program is conducted primarily in classrooms in the store. New hires are familiarized with the use of cash registers, customer service and safety rules, company benefits, and so forth. Four to six of these 22 hours are spent on the sales floor. Following this training period, new employees are placed in a Grade 1 position.

Grade 1 positions—the lowest grade in the job-classification ladder for nonexempt employees—account for the largest share of the sales staff. These classifications correspond to sales positions involving a cashier-only job and are found in departments where service is left entirely to the customer and where product information is nil, for example, in the greeting cards department. New employees are evaluated at the end of the first 30 days, 60 days, 90 days, and six months after starting. The probationary period is usually 90 days. After six months of employment, the employee is eligible for the first pay increase and then every year on the anniversary of her or his hiring following an annual evaluation. (For example, in the Albany, New York area in early 1982, the entry wage rate was $4.70 per hour, with annual increases ranging from $0.25 to $0.75 per hour.) At a minimum, new employees remain in their initial Grade 1 assignment for 18 months. On average, within the first 18 to 36 months, new employees are recommended for what is called a *better job*, usually corresponding to a favored schedule, an interesting department, or a better grade.

The next level in the nonexempt job hierarchy is a Grade 2 position. In the jargon of the company, Grade 2 positions are "semitechnical." Employees can learn the job rather quickly, but there is more service required from the sales clerk, who must narrow the range of the customer's choice. Grade 2 positions are found, for example, in departments such as china and silverware, cameras, and women's suits or ready-to-wear. Most of the training associated with such positions is provided by the vendors themselves. For women's garments, for example, once a year, or more often, vendors organize a one- or two-day training session to introduce new lines of goods to the sales staff. Typically these sessions involve a specialized fashion show held either in the store itself or nearby and paid for by manufacturers.

At the next promotional level are Grade 3 positions, jobs which require a good bit of knowledge and service. These are found in high-ticket departments: furniture; major home appliances; men's clothing, such as suits; bedding; floor covering; or bridal. They are essentially the old commissioned sales jobs. They pay well and are usually staffed with long-time employees.

Finally, in a number of departments, successful sales clerks can move up to become *lead sales* (otherwise called senior sales, yellow sales, or expeditors). Lead sales have a training function, are people who have seniority, provide continuity as sales managers move around, have some authority over the sales staff, and have a say in evaluating performances (primarily from a technical standpoint). In the past, a lead sales position was used as a ladder to move from nonexempt to exempt levels. The introduction of the orbit system ended this role, placing very much in question the existence of the position (more on this later).

As noted previously, the third and last major change among sales staff was in the sex-race-age composition of the personnel. Until the mid–1960s, an overwhelming number of sales clerks had been white women who were 30 years and older. In the New York area, the company was known for its relatively good record in employing minorities, although by the company's own admission, there was a tendency for its black employees to be "ghettoized" in certain occupations (porter, elevator attendant, etc.). By the early 1970s, however, because of the competitive efforts of other employers in hiring mature women and because of the major push for EEO, the company, like many of its competitors, began reaching out to new pools of workers, primarily to minorities and youth. Later in the chapter, I return to the shift in the racial composition of the company's labor force. Here, however, it is useful to note the shift to youth which, while less well documented, has been nevertheless dramatic. For example, according to one of the executives interviewed, in 1981 the company opened a new store in the San Francisco Bay Area in which all sales clerks were under 28 years of age. According to the same executive, in 1982 the share of sales employees 18 years or younger ranged from approximately 7 to 12 percent in late 1982, depending on the store.

Staffing the Supporting Areas

While the supporting areas are characterized by a much greater proportion of full-time, nonexempt employees, promotional opportunities are fairly similar to those for employees on the sales floor. For example, R. H. Macy & Co. has five distribution centers—one for each division and a specialized distribution center for ready to wear shared by Macy's

New York and Bamberger's. Each center is staffed with a small core of full-time employees, all in supervisory positions (senior markers, senior stock clerks), with a morning and afternoon shift of part-time, lower-level employees. The traditional line of promotion is from low-level staff to supervisor, implying a shift from part-time to full-time work.

The Impact of Technological Change on Employment

The argument thus far has been that the introduction of the orbit system and the concomitant transformation of the company's personnel organization resulted from changes that originated in an intensively competitive marketplace. Clearly, technological changes had little to do with the dimensions of transformation highlighted thus far. Nevertheless, technological changes did occur, with implications for jobs and skills. Close examination suggests a rather limited direct impact by new technologies on the sales areas but a substantial impact on back-of-the-store activities.

Technological Change in Sales

While the introduction of electronic cash registers permitted productivity gains in areas of inventory control (stockrooms, receiving and shipping docks) modernized earlier with ticket-sorting equipment and mainframe computer technologies, this new technology, however, like earlier ones, did not affect fundamentally the staffing of sales areas. As noted previously, the move toward greater customer self-service and the trend toward greater use of part-time employees led both to major productivity gains (see Table 3.6), but they occurred largely as a response to competition, not to technology per se.

Still, the computerization of the payment and inventory recording process helped produce information that management was able to use to better staff the stores. On the one hand, electronic cash registers helped create detailed profiles of customer traffic patterns through departments, which stores were able to use to adjust sales staffing to traffic needs. On the other hand, advanced computerization made it easier to maintain employee records, collect time sheets, and produce paychecks, all of which simplified the record-keeping operations which grew as a result of the increasing use of part-time workers.

In addition, the introduction of electronic cash registers made it possible for sales clerks to investigate a customer's credit status prior to a transaction, which, in turn, allowed the company to expand the

TABLE 3.6

Trends in Employment and Output (all divisions): R. H. Macy & Co., 1947–1980

	1947	1951	1960	1970	1980
Year-Round Employees (full-time, part-time, and short-hour)[a]	20,500	24,000	28,000	38,000	45,000
Sales ($ mil.)	285	351	509	907	2,374
Number of Stores	13	18	36	63	89
Total Square Footage (in thousands of sq. ft.)	5,263	6,843	9,873	18,378	20,926
Square Feet per Year-Round Employee	257	281	353	403	465
Sales per Year-Round Employee (real $)	13,942	14,618	18,179	23,869	52,745
Sales per Year-Round Employee (constant 1967 $)[b]	17,829	16,977	20,289	20,559	29,565

[a] Excludes Christmas part-time hires (approximately 10,000 employees).
[b] Based on consumer price index for apparel and upkeep.

Source: R. H. Macy & Co., *Annual Reports,* 1947, 1951, 1960, 1970, and 1980.

distribution of charge cards without increasing substantially its financial risks.

Technological Changes in Supporting Areas

Back of the store, the introduction of electronic data processing had a direct impact on the work process. Several areas deserve special emphasis.

In the areas of distribution and inventory control, R. H. Macy & Co., like its competitors, benefited tremendously from the introduction of automated warehousing and computerized inventory control technologies. In general, these technologies did away with the need for large numbers of stock clerks, shipping clerks, and similar employees. While I did not get specific figures for R. H. Macy & Co., at J. C. Penney for example, one executive reported that the shift to on-line inventory control had allowed his company to lower the average number of in-store stock clerks from 20 to 30 to two to three employees per store! In addition, improved warehousing and inventory control methods helped reduce greatly the costs of space needed for inventory storage. Today's average branch store in the department store industry is about 160,000 square feet compared to 250,000 square feet five years ago, but the ratio of selling to nonselling space has gone up from roughly 55 percent to 75 to 80 percent. R. H. Macy & Co.'s newest branches remain slightly larger than those of competitors, roughly in the 200,000 square feet range, but yet are smaller than branches built earlier (*Moody's Industrial Manual*, 1981). Simply, with advanced computerization, the distribution centers, rather than the branches, carry most of the stores' inventory.

In the areas of financial control, account processing, and billing R. H. Macy & Co. benefited from electronic data processing in ways similar to other industries. Earlier on, a great deal of the work of the firm's financial offices was basic bookkeeping and number crunching, necessitating large numbers of clericals and low-level bookkeepers. Basic data processing, though, has become increasingly automated, and much of the data-entry process has been relegated to warehouses where scanners record entries or to sales floors where electronic cash registers recorded customer transactions directly into computers (or into computer-readable form). As a result, work in central offices has become relatively more investigative and analytic and less involved with data entry or processing. Progressively, these changes have shifted the balance of skills toward higher-skilled personnel.

It is in the area of merchandising, however, that the impact of new technology has been perhaps the most significant. In the late 1950s and 1960s, a good part of the buyer's job involved tracking how fast classifications were moving through departments and, in most instances, outguessing what was really happening; sales clerks could not keep up with the frequency or the level of detail which the buyer needed to place new orders intelligently. The introduction of electronic data processing was a fundamental step forward in transforming the merchandising function. With the system in place today, company buyers receive a computer printout every morning showing the status of stock and the sales velocity of classifications. Hence, while the introduction of the orbit system has refocused the efforts of buyers on buying and merchandising, technology has relieved buyers from most record-keeping operations associated with buying. Buyers can devote more time and energy to "merchandising" now that the complexity of the "merchandising" function has increased due to a multiplication of options within product classifications, the shortening of product fads and fashions, and the increasing importance of imports.

Finally, at the time this case analysis was carried out, R. H. Macy & Co. was working on the introduction of an on-line computerized ordering system linking its buyers to suppliers. The company hoped that this new system would improve greatly the efficiency of shipping and distributing goods and further eliminate time spent by buyers on paper-handling tasks.

Implications of Organizational and Technological Changes for Employment Opportunities

Employment Growth: Numbers and Types of Jobs Created

As shown in Table 3.6, between 1947 and 1980, the number of R. H. Macy & Co.'s year-round employees more than doubled, from slightly fewer than 21,000 to about 45,000, while sales grew more than eight times in current dollars, from about $300 million to $2.4 billion (approximately a fourfold increase in constant dollars). Productivity grew slowly during the 1950s and 1960s but was followed by a whopping 50 percent increase during the 1970s: in constant dollars, from about $20,500 per year-round employee in 1970 to $29,500 in 1980. This suggests that the changes in personnel organization which accompanied the introduction of the orbit system did indeed translate into major productivity gains.

Similar trends have continued in the early 1980s. In existing stores, there have been few net additions to the total pool of jobs, even though each store continues to offer large numbers of openings resulting from the normal process of employee turnover. Increases in sales volume have come mostly from continued productivity increases and new net employment growth, mostly from expansion into new markets. In particular, Bamberger's has pushed the borders of its market further south, mostly into Maryland and the suburbs of Washington, D.C., and Macy's New York has begun moving into Florida and Texas.

One marked change consistent with the earlier discussion of technology has been a continuing occupational shift. Between 1966 and 1982, the number of sales clerks grew at a rate roughly similar to that of total employment. By comparison, the number of managers and professionals grew much faster and that of clerical workers, operatives, laborers, and service workers much slower, reflecting a shift in the supporting areas away from lower-level positions toward higher-level positions (see Table 3.7).

Opportunities for Internal Promotion

The introduction of the orbit system has affected opportunities for internal promotion in two roughly opposite ways.

Among executives (a small but relatively fast-growing share of employment), the orbit system has been aimed at improving and speeding the process of mobility so that few employees with the proper qualifications and a substantial interest in the business remain stuck in low-level management positions. At the same time, however, the orbit system

TABLE 3.7
R. H. Macy & Co.'s Changing Occupational Distribution, 1966–1982

	1982 (#)	1966 (#)	1966–1982 (% change)	1982 (%)	1966 (%)
Officials and Managers	6,085	3,037	100.4	12.5	8.1
Professionals	1,130	758	49.1	2.3	2.0
Technicians	97	106	−8.5	0.2	0.3
Sales Workers	25,568	19,388	31.9	52.7	51.6
Clerical Workers	7,060	6,869	2.8	14.5	18.3
Craft Workers	528	309	70.9	1.1	0.8
Operatives	217	343	−36.7	0.4	0.9
Laborers	661	561	17.8	1.4	1.5
Service Workers	7,188	6,194	16.1	14.8	16.5
Total	48,550	37,565	29.2	100.0	100.0

Source: R. H. Macy & Co., *EEO-1 Reports,* 1966 and 1972.

has broken the old mobility ladder from "nonexempt" to "exempt" ranks, so that rank-and-file employees who could once aspire to reaching supervisory or middle-managerial positions now find themselves locked out. Some laddering among nonexempt ranks has remained, but it has become very limited. By now, the bulk of internal mobility opportunities has been restricted to a new class of workers who enter the executive ladder straight out of college.

Skills

While the transformation of R. H. Macy & Co. suggests a sharper division among functional areas, it does not reflect necessarily a relative downgrading of skills. The introduction of advanced electronic data processing has done much to eliminate the drudgery once associated with record-keeping and data processing and to shift the emphasis of skills toward other areas, particularly product and market knowledge.

For executives, the new technology has eliminated part of the need for managing record-keeping and has provided additional time and better data for problem-solving tasks. This was noted earlier for buyers, who can now devote more time to merchandising, but the same can be said for other executives throughout the organizations.

For sales clerks, the introduction of electronic data processing technology has had a somewhat similar impact. Electronic cash registers have simplified or eliminated traditional accounting and record-keeping

TABLE 3.8
Employee Tenure in the Department Store Industry, 1950s–1970s (in percentages)

	Working at Least 3 Years	Working 1 Year or Less
1950s	42.4	18.9
1960s	34.7	25.1
1970s	31.7	27.0

Source: Barry Bluestone, Patricia Hanna, Sarah Kuhn, and Laura Moore, *The Retail Revolution* (Boston: Auburn House, 1981).

tasks handled at the department level and have given employees time to familiarize themselves with the growing diversity and complexity of product classifications. There is evidence that the company has an increasing need for on-the-job training to help sales clerks become familiar with the growing array of product characteristics and options facing customers.

Stability of Employment

Among exempt employees, the company emphasizes strong executive attachment to the firm. The shuffling of young executives through the orbit system is designed to promote attachment. This may be somewhat unusual for an industry in which turnover among buyers is known to be quite high.

In terms of nonexempt employees, however, R. H. Macy & Co. follows the industry's pattern. The company relies increasingly on part-time employment not only because such a pattern makes it easier to adjust staffing resources to traffic patterns or to the increasing number of business hours but because it permits the firm to limit its commitment (and the related costs) to a large number of employees.

The impact of this reduced commitment can be seen in the evolution of turnover ratios in the industry. In their research on the department store industry, Bluestone et al. (1981) found that employee turnover increased steadily throughout the postwar period. Annual gross separation rates for the department store industry grew from the 36 to 41 percent range in the late 1950s to the 41 to 45 percent range in the mid–1960s and to the 47 to 51 percent range in the early 1970s. This change is also underscored by estimates of workers' tenure in the department store industry shown in Table 3.8. Between the 1950s and the 1970s, the proportion of employees working three years or more in the industry decreased from a 42 to a 32 percent average, while the proportion of those working one year or less increased from a 19 to a 27 percent average. The lack of appropriate data makes it impossible to measure the equivalent ratios for R. H. Macy & Co. Most likely, however, the company's recent experience has followed the industry's pattern.

Barriers to Entry: Sex and Race Composition

Like most firms in its industry, the company's hiring practices have changed markedly in the past two decades, especially in regard to women, minorities, and youth. In terms of women and minorities, the change has come partly in response to the nation's concern for EEO. Table 3.9, on the firm's EEO–1 reports for the earliest and latest available years (1982 and 1966), shows basic changes in the sex-race occupational composition of the company (large employers must file EEO–1 reports each year with the EEO-C).

Two key observations are warranted. First, R. H. Macy & Co. has traditionally been a large employer of women. For that matter, the share of women has even increased in recent years, from 69.6 percent of its labor force in 1966 to 73.5 percent in 1982, in part because accelerated recruiting among minorities has been biased toward minority women. Nevertheless, on the company's own admission, the company did tend to segregate women in lower-level occupations (sales and clericals) in the past and has had to make major efforts to break down some of these barriers. The partial results of these efforts are shown in Table 3.8 in the sizable relative gains made by white women in managerial and professional occupations between 1966 and 1982. According to executives interviewed, while buyer positions were the highest echelons that women could previously be expected to reach, women are now actively sought in higher-level positions, although the full impact of this policy has yet to be felt at the top corporate echelons. Still, while most store managers in the past were men, today a majority are women.

Second, compared to other firms or industries, the company has long been a large employer of minorities. Still, relative to the composition of its own labor force and despite progress in recent years, the Macy company continues to trail in its placement of minorities of both sexes in three of its five most important occupations—sales workers, professionals and officials, and managers. Traditionally, minority females at R. H. Macy & Co. fared best in office clerical or service-worker positions, and minority males did well in service-worker jobs and in the relatively unimportant craft, operative, and laborer positions. Executives at R. H. Macy & Co. point out that in bringing minorities into professional and managerial positions, the retail industry, being neither a high-paying

TABLE 3.9
Occupational Distribution of Major Groups of Workers: R. H. Macy & Co., 1982 and 1966

	1982					1966				
	Occupation as % of All Labor Force	Major Sex-Race Group as % Employment in Occupation[a]				Occupation as % of All Labor Force	Major Sex-Race Group as % Employment in Occupation[a]			
		White Male	White Female	Minority Male	Minority Female		White Male	White Female	Minority Male	Minority Female
Officials & Managers	12.5	36.4	54.6	3.5	5.5	8.1	56.3	40.5	2.3	0.9
Professionals	2.3	32.0	51.8	4.8	11.1	2.0	48.5	47.6	2.0	0.9
Technicians	0.2	23.7	54.6	14.5	11.2	0.3	32.1	63.2	1.9	2.8
Sales Workers	52.7	12.6	70.0	3.0	14.4	51.6	17.2	74.8	1.3	5.7
Office Clerical	14.5	8.1	55.1	5.4	31.4	18.3	10.6	68.0	2.7	18.7
Craft Workers	1.1	84.0	6.8	7.7	1.5	0.8	96.4	0.0	2.9	0.0
Operatives	0.4	48.4	7.8	34.1	9.7	0.9	28.3	22.5	20.7	18.1
Laborers	1.4	66.6	3.0	28.7	1.7	1.5	51.7	0.0	22.8	0.0
Service Workers	14.8	31.8	32.1	21.0	15.1	16.5	35.1	30.2	23.5	13.2
All Occupations	100.0	19.9	58.0	6.6	15.5	100.0	25.0	60.6	5.5	9.9

[a] Each line adds to 100 percent.

Occupational Overrepresentation or Underrepresentation of Major Groups of Workers: R. H. Macy & Co., 1982 and 1966

	1982				1966			
	White Male	White Female	Minority Male	Minority Female	White Male	White Female	Minority Male	Minority Female
Officials & Managers	1.83	0.94	0.53	0.35	2.25	0.67	0.42	0.09
Professionals	1.61	0.89	0.73	0.72	1.94	0.79	0.36	0.09
Technicians	1.19	0.94	2.20	0.72	1.28	1.04	0.35	0.28
Sales Workers	0.63	1.21	0.45	0.93	0.69	1.23	0.24	0.58
Office Clerical	0.41	0.95	0.82	2.03	0.42	1.12	0.49	1.89
Craft Workers	4.22	0.12	1.17	0.10	3.86	0.00	0.53	0.00
Operatives	2.43	0.13	5.17	0.63	1.13	0.37	3.76	1.83
Laborers	3.35	0.05	4.35	0.11	2.07	0.00	4.15	0.00
Service Workers	1.60	0.55	3.18	0.97	1.40	0.50	4.27	1.33

Note: The four principal occupational groups are underlined for emphasis. The index of representation is measured as the ratio of the share of employment of a major group in a given occupation divided by its share of all employment. A ratio above 1 indicates overrepresentation; below 1, underrepresentation.

Source: R. H. Macy & Co., EEO-1 Reports, 1966 and 1972.

nor a glamorous industry, suffers from competition for the too few educated minorities with those industries that are more attractive and better paying.

Barrier to Entry: Education

Like other employers, the company has responded to the widespread expansion of higher education by moving toward a two-tier hiring structure separated by a college education: college graduates are recruited to enter at the lower-level executive echelons, while others start in entry-level nonexempt staff positions. In recent years the company has done some hiring in the external labor market to staff some of its highest sales positions. This effort has focused mostly on graduates from vocational schools or two-year community colleges or on experienced sales workers from other firms. These new recruits have been placed in lead sales positions or Grade 3 positions in high-ticket departments.

Until recently, the company had shied away from hiring graduates from business administration and other professional schools largely because such people command too much money in the marketplace and because the entry level in the orbit structure was set at a lower level. Nevertheless, in response to the increasing importance of higher-level specialized corporate functions, such as finance, legal counsel, and data processing, the company has done limited recruiting among graduates from professional schools, especially since the late 1970s.

At the nonexempt level, the company requires at a minimum a high school diploma. Hiring is done at the store level, and many of the new recruits come to the company through informal recruiting by Macy employees and their social networks. The company does not use newspaper classified advertising. When the need exists, special outreach programs are launched. For example, in the past when several of the Macy's New York suburban branches experienced shortages, several store managers opened new channels of access to women by initiating a Second-Career Program for suburban housewives. The program involved presentations to women's clubs, church groups, and so forth. Also in the New York area, the Macy company, along with other firms, has been involved since the late 1960s in the youth co-op program. This program establishes special relationships between a New York employer and the area's high schools, with the firm providing part-time employment to students during the school year. R. H. Macy & Co. uses these youngsters usually in janitorial or sales support jobs, rarely in sales positions. Many, however, stay with the Macy company past graduation.

Earnings

The last major attribute of employment opportunities involves earnings. In the absence of company data, some indirect insights can be gained by reviewing industry data.

The study by Bluestone et al. (1981) points to some of the basic patterns. In general, retail remains a poor-paying industry relative to others. Bluestone and his colleagues found that the average wage for year-round (full- and part-time) male employees was barely more than $6,800 annually in 1975, $2,800 for female employees. They also found sharp differences by race and age, with blacks, other minorities, and youths faring even worse than the averages indicated earlier.

In addition, when reviewing the evolution of earnings distribution by sex for year-round workers in the New England department store industry, Bluestone et al. found sharp changes between 1957 and 1975 (see Figure 3.5). From a unimodal distribution of earnings in 1957, with the peak for men slightly higher than that for females, the earnings distribution turned highly dualistic for men by 1975 but not for women. This reflected a new pattern in which most women and some groups of men (especially minority or younger men) were being confined to the new, low-paying, part-time employment (sales clerks, service workers, office clericals), while a small group of mostly white men controlled access to well-paid managerial and professional positions.

In the absence of company data but based on earlier observations about the company's occupational distribution by sex, it would seem safe to assume that a similar bimodality of earnings exists at R. H. Macy & Co., although in this case involving a growing number of women in the high earnings bracket. One executive reported annual salaries for female store managers in the $70,000 range in 1981.

Ongoing Personnel Changes

The tremendous success of the company over the past decade does not mean that recent years have been problem-free. There have been new tensions, and these tensions are interesting to examine since they shed some light on the difficulties associated with managing the new human resource organization.

Nonexempt Personnel

In recent years, R. H. Macy & Co. has become concerned about sustaining the productivity advances of the late 1960s and the 1970s.

The reorganization of staffing in sales after the mid–1960s was oriented toward maximizing sales output per employee while containing labor

FIGURE 3.5
Earnings Distribution for Year-Round Workers
in the New England Department Store Industry, 1957 and 1975

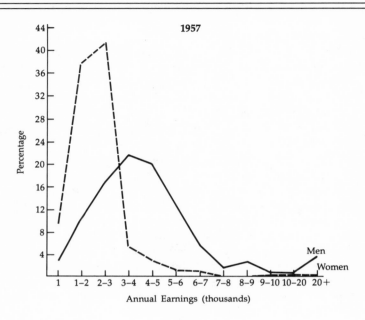

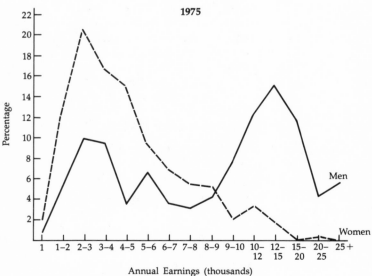

Source: Barry Bluestone, Patricia Hanna, Sarah Kuhn, and Laura Moore, *The Retail Revolution* (Boston: Auburn House, 1981).

costs. But the emphasis on limited sales force attachment to the company has tended to run counter to the level of employee involvement needed to maintain high standards of work quality. Quality needs to be restored if productivity is to rise again. This parallels the company's need both for reemphasizing service as part of its upscaling strategy and for adding qualified sales personnel because the trend toward multiplication of product classifications has rendered the sales task a more demanding one than in the past.

One executive suggests that Macy's should consider doing more in the way of participative management:

> As an industry, we have done very little by way of 'participative management.' But we could do a lot more. The setting is perfect. We used to promise upward mobility, but we do not any longer. We have to be able to give something else. We have tried quality control circles in some of our stores, but we haven't really tried very hard. Remember that under the old system, buyers used to hold department meetings every day. But it is no longer the case. Buyers buy for sixteen stores or more. All they do is check a computer printout every morning and no one ever bothers to go ask sales people why things don't sell.

> We need much greater involvement of sales clerks. There is a malaise which needs to be alleviated; we need to boost productivity, but people are bored with their jobs and with the prospect of staying thirty years in the same jobs.

Others suggest that the time might have come for the company to move away from part-time employment.

Related to the above issue is an ongoing debate about reintroducing an extensive sales commission system. Sales commission used to apply primarily to sales people in high-ticket departments (mostly in what today are called Grade 3 positions). In 1968 Bamberger's first moved to a complete elimination of the commission system in some of its stores. With the commission system, buyers were complaining that they had no control over the amount of goods sold. With commissions being determined as a fixed ratio of the sales price, salespeople in high-ticket departments could easily earn good money without pushing. In addition, the 1969–1971 recession made the regular fixed-paycheck system seem attractive to some of the commissioned sales clerks because of its recession-proof nature. By the early 1970s, commissions had been eliminated in most of the nonunion stores and preserved only in certain departments in union stores. By the late 1970s, there was a push to have the system reinstated; today, R. H. Macy & Co. operates a system halfway between the fixed salary and the commission system. The company keeps a record of individual sales clerks' transactions, a job rendered easier by advanced electronic data processing. At the end of the year, the company produces a detailed tabulation of how much sales clerks would have made under the commission system. If their salary is way below, it is adjusted upward; if the salary is way above, it can be adjusted downward but only after two consecutive years (this to account for recessions).

Junior Executives

Another source of concern among company executives focuses on the middle layers of management. By design, today's two-tiered employment structure makes for very high turnover in low-level management positions to avoid clogging up middle-level positions at a high cost to the company.

But high turnover has its problems too. The lack of continuity among department managers makes for poor overall supervision of departments. Some executives argue that the company needs to bring back static employees (i.e. people who do not move upward) in middle-management positions. In recent years, Bamberger's has tried this solution by promoting a few sales people to lead sales and/or department manager positions. In one of its stores, it has been trying out a system in which a number of people with a two-year college degree enter at a level lower than that of department manager (e.g., in a lead sales position) and are then allowed to move up more slowly. Other executives of the firm argue in favor of a more aggressive introduction of quality circles as a way to filter down some supervisory functions.

Senior Executives

A last concern of the company is directed to its need to staff special functions, such as finance or data processing, whose importance has been growing. In the past, these positions tended to be filled through ad hoc outside recruiting or the internal promotion of managers. Increasingly, however, the company is being forced to do regular recruiting of high-level professionals. With this change has come the realization that the drive and aspirations of highly professional personnel may not only differ sharply from those of the buyers and store managers but may not be easily fulfilled within the Macy organization.

In short, these are among some of the tensions that have surfaced in recent years and that are partly a product of the changes that were introduced in the mid- to late 1960s. In fact, however, these problems are not unique to R. H. Macy & Co. Evident in many organizations, these concerns simply reflect the tensions between the old and the new labor markets. I return to these issues in Chapters 6 and 7.

Notes

1. "The Cellar" had been introduced earlier at Bamberger's and Macy's California.

2. For example, sheets used to come in three sizes (cot, twin, and double), one color (white), and two materials (percale and muslin), that is, in six basic options. Today, sheets are available in four sizes (single, double, queen, and king), two fits (flat or fitted), several qualities of material (usually, various mixes of cotton and polyester), and a multiplicity of colors, prints, and patterns, making for dozens of options.

3. Like others in the industry, the company also employs very large numbers of temporary employees for the Christmas season (somewhere around 10,000 employees compared to a year-round labor force of 52,000). According to the company, these are mostly people interested in getting income for this traditionally high-spending season and in benefiting from discounts granted by the company to its employees. Few are interested in long-term attachment to the firm, although some use the opportunity to make their way into the full-year labor force.

4

Utilities: The Case of New York Telephone

Once a subsidiary of American Telephone & Telegraph (AT&T), today a principal division of NYNEX, one of the independent Bell Operating Companies (BOC) created in the wake of the dismantling of the old AT&T, New York Telephone has long been at the forefront of change in the telephone industry. With New York City and its surroundings as principal markets, change at the company has often arrived earlier than at other Bell subsidiaries.

Still, change at New York Telephone has come against the background of twenty years of radical transformation in U.S. telecommunications. As early as the mid- and late 1960s, growing demand for data telecommunications services from commercial customers was putting considerable pressure on AT&T to modernize its systems with new computerized technologies. In addition, developments in telecommunications technology was fueling demand from other firms to be allowed to enter the telecommunications field and compete with Ma Bell. These and other pressures led to the first steps in the regulatory dismantling of the old AT&T. Ultimately, this process found its conclusion in the 1982 consent decree between AT&T and the Justice Department in which AT&T agreed to dismantle its former monopoly.

As these developments unfolded, each with major challenges to human resource policies and practices, AT&T found itself caught in a major conflict with the EEO-C regarding the company's affirmative action record. The 1973 AT&T-EEO-C consent decree established new employment rules for the company that would remain in effect until 1979 and that would further constrain the way in which AT&T could resolve its human resource problems.

At New York Telephone, the impact of the nationwide changes affecting the entire Bell system was further compounded by specific local conditions. In the late 1960s, New York Telephone faced a particularly rapid rise in demand linked to both the rapid growth of office-based activity in Manhattan and a large rise in demand for residential service. These events occurred while profits eroded, and the company was forced to cut down on investment and the improvement and repair of equipment.

The first phase of a massive corrective capital investment program (1969–1971) was followed by an eight-month strike by New York Telephone unions (July 1971–February 1972) and shortly thereafter by the introduction of an extensive affirmative action program in response to the AT&T-EEO-C consent decree (1973). The following years saw major adjustments in the company's use of human resources. The phaseout of the EEO consent decree after 1979 broadened the extent to which the company could respond to change, leading to yet further alterations in its management of human resources in the late 1970s and early 1980s.

This chapter documents the national and local changes that have affected New York Telephone over the past 15 to 20 years and analyzes in detail the impact of these changes on the company's human resource organization both during and after the AT&T-EEO-C consent decree.

Twenty Years of Change in the Telecommunications Industry: 1965–1985

While it is easy to remember the trauma, apprehension, and uncertainty that gripped the nation's telephone consumers in the wake of the dismantling of AT&T's monopoly on January 1, 1984, it is important to recall that this development marked the conclusion of nearly twenty years of change in the industry resulting from growth in demand, deregulation, new technologies, and a new emphasis on competition.

Growth in Demand

In the late 1960s, AT&T was faced with a sharp rise in demand for conventional telephone services (voice messages) from both residential and business customers. Between 1965 and 1975, the number of Bell-installed telephones grew more than 40 percent (from 79 to 112 million sets), the number of Bell central offices increased 30 percent (from 13,425 to 17,232), and wire mileage almost doubled (from 423 to 832 million miles) in an effort to meet a 65 percent increase in the average number of daily telephone calls (from 273 to 448 million) (U.S. Federal Communications Commission).

In addition, this growth was accompanied by a shift in the type of service demanded, from the transmission of voice messages to the transmission of data. While confined primarily to a few large cities such

TABLE 4.2
AT&T Labor Force, December 31, 1973–January 15, 1979

	1973	1979	Percent Change
Total White Collar	552,990	568,113	2.8
Officials and Managers	164,438	191,436	16.4
Administrative	30,135	33,913	12.5
Sales Workers	7,038	8,999	27.9
Clerical	207,461	231,111	11.4
Operators	143,918	102,654	−28.7
Total Blue Collar	257,592	243,739	−5.4
Outside Crafts	136,391	135,072	−1.0
Inside Crafts	97,198	97,569	0.4
Service Workers	24,003	11,098	−53.8
Total Employment	810,582	811,852	0.2

Source: AT&T, *EEO-1 Reports,* 1973 and 1979; Herbert R. Northrup and John A. Larson, *The Impact of the AT&T-EEO Consent Decree,* Labor Relations and Public Policy Series, vol. 20 (Philadelphia: University of Pennsylvania, 1979).

Competition and Marketing

A last major area in which the shift in demand and rising competition forced AT&T to change its conventional method of doing business was sales and marketing. As a result of their monopolistic protection from competition, both AT&T and its local subsidiaries entered the 1970s with weak marketing and sales organizations. Organized along functional lines, the Bell companies were essentially engineering-oriented companies, with the *outside* and *inside* craft departments (including, respectively, line and telephone installation and repair, and switch installation and maintenance) as the elite departments of the companies. Ineluctably, however, the challenge of competition forced AT&T to build up its marketing and sales staffs, mostly in the local operating companies.

The impact of the aforementioned forces of change on AT&T's labor force can readily be seen in the employment shifts among major occupational groups between 1973 and 1979 (see Table 4.2). During a period when AT&T total employment remained roughly unchanged, the number of telephone operators declined by almost one-third, the number of craftsmen stagnated, and the number of sales workers, administrative staff, and officials and managers increased rapidly due, in part at least, to the buildup of the marketing organization.

**Unscrambling the Crisis
at New York Telephone: 1969–1972**

In which way did the course of transformation differ at New York Telephone from the rest of AT&T? Clearly, New York Telephone was influenced by the broad changes affecting AT&T throughout this long period. Yet, for reasons specific to the New York company, changes occasionally became especially dramatic. In particular, events that took place between 1969 and 1972 had a major impact on the following decade.

The 1960s: The Mounting Crisis

The late 1960s saw a steady erosion of New York Telephone profits. The company claimed, at the time, that this resulted from operating through most of the 1960s without a rate increase. As profits diminished, the company cut back on investment and maintenance. Meanwhile, New York Telephone was confronted with a surge in demand resulting from several factors, including the certification of telephone bills as a welfare expense,[1] Manhattan's office construction boom, and the surge of activity on Wall Street. In a period of two to three years, the company added over one million residences and businesses to its list of customers.

The results were traumatic. By the late 1960s, New York Telephone was afflicted by a major service breakdown. There were long waiting lists for phone installation and repair, and due to the overloading of central offices, switches, and transmission cables, customers encountered difficulties in making and completing calls.

Compounding these problems was the company's shortage of employees in an extremely tight labor market. In addition, the unions were using this opportunity to put pressure on the company, partly because salaries and wages were lower than those paid by other utilities. The result was high turnover among employees and a relatively inexperienced work force.

Unscrambling the Crisis

To remedy the situation, New York Telephone needed substantial new investments. Given the weakness of its financial position, the company had to call on its parent for huge infusions of funds. Between 1969 and

1970, the annual capital investment program of New York Telephone jumped 100 percent, from $500 million to $1 billion. In 1970 the executive in charge of New York Telephone's new construction program estimated that the company would need to invest over $10 billion in the coming decade. In the end, New York Telephone invested well over that amount (*Moody's Public Utility Manuals*).

In addition to money, New York Telephone needed equipment. Given the company's insufficient needs assessment in the late 1960s, it had to petition for help from Western Electric, which agreed to divert to New York Telephone equipment earmarked for other subsidiaries.

Between 1969 and 1971, New York Telephone installed a considerable amount of new switching equipment. It did so by performing engineering marvels, lowering the normal lapse time between conception and operation of new switches from approximately three years to an average of nearly 18 months.

Meanwhile, tension was building among the company, its employees and the unions. Contractually, the major issues were pay increases and the excessive use of overtime in certain departments. In addition, although not directly reflected in company-union negotiations, there were simmering tensions on issues related to the impact of the new switches on future work and employment.

The 1971–1972 Strike

Nineteen-seventy-one was a year for companywide labor negotiations at AT&T. Negotiations took place throughout the summer. A new contract was established in early July 1971 and ratified on July 21 by all subsidiaries, except New York Telephone (U.S. Department of Labor, 1980).

New York Telephone employees struck that same day, believing that the company was in a weak position and would settle rapidly. Instead, the strike continued until February 16, 1972, by which time the unions had lost badly. Not only had the unions been unable to extract major new concessions, but they had given the company eight months of free rein during which managers and supervisors had made major adjustments and changes in the operation of some of the new equipment.

By the summer of 1971, a great deal of new switching equipment was already in place. What was needed was mostly start-up and fine-tuning. Under normal operating conditions, this would have been done by craft employees. Given contractual work rules prevailing at the time and some of the problems then faced by New York Telephone, such as the high turnover among inexperienced craftsmen and the reluctance to hire and train minority males, fine-tuning and start-up could have been a long, protracted process. Instead, because of the strike, management was able to move in and expedite the process. Every weekend for the duration of the strike, AT&T dispatched planeloads of managers, engineers, and supervisors from other operating subsidiaries to lend a hand. Between September 1971 and February 1972, New York Telephone managers not only put most of the new equipment in operation but installed 700,000 new telephones throughout New York State! By the time union members returned to their jobs, a considerable amount of work had been accomplished, much had been learned by managers and supervisors, and informal new standards and work rules had been established.

The Aftermath

From a technical standpoint, New York Telephone had accomplished a turnaround by early 1973. In less than five years, the physical plant had been greatly upgraded. For example, the 17 switching locations in Manhattan, plus many in the outer boroughs, had been rebuilt. In addition, the company had poured millions of dollars into the upgrading of its repair shops, garages, and fleets.

From a personnel standpoint, New York Telephone managers left the 1971–1972 crisis very aware of the need to reduce employment in certain functional areas. In 1972 there were 106,000 employees (historical peak). Five years later, the company had trimmed its work force by over 25 percent, to 75,000 employees. Company officials assert that most of the trimming was done through attrition and by "closing down" the hiring office, a point sharply debated by the unions that argue that numerous layoffs were initiated, even though they may have been disguised. In general, New York Telephone executives became increasingly aware of the need to shift craftsmen and operators out of central offices as the business became more and more capital-intensive and to expand the marketing and commercial organization of the company. The company began experimenting with a system of lateral ladders to shift people away from declining departments or occupations into growing ones, for example, shifting employees out of operator positions in central offices into business representative positions in the commercial department. This system of lateral ladders was the forerunner of a similar, although more sophisticated, Upgrade and Transfer Plan (UTP) that was to be introduced following the AT&T-EEO-C consent decree in 1973.

The 1973 AT&T-EEO-C Consent Decree

The last observation points to yet another axis of change which would impact profoundly New York Telephone's personnel organization: the advent of the 1973 AT&T-EEO-C consent decree. While AT&T had begun negotiating an affirmative action strategy with the EEO-C as early as 1967, it took nearly six years to conclude the complex litigation involving AT&T, the EEO-C, the U.S. Department of Labor, the FCC, several other federal agencies, and various groups such as the National Association for the Advancement of Colored People (NAACP), the National Organization of Women (NOW), and the American Civil Liberties Union (ACLU). On January 18, 1973, AT&T and the EEO-C agreed to settle out of court with what came to be known as the 1973 AT&T-EEO-C consent decree (Northrup and Larson, 1979).

The affirmative action plan developed by AT&T to meet EEO goals is discussed in greater detail later in this chapter, but two preliminary observations must be made. First, the plan developed by AT&T and the EEO-C was influenced by some of the other axes of change discussed earlier in this chapter since their impact on the company's labor force also needed to be taken into account. Second, the original affirmative action plan remained in effect only until 1979. While AT&T and its subsidiaries were forced to abide by the basic principles of the consent decree after 1979, they were able to regain some latitude in managing differently some of the features of the original affirmative action plan. This happened at a time when the pressure from emerging competitors in both the equipment and service fields was beginning to be felt heavily. The implications, as I show at the end of the chapter, were profound in weakening an internal labor market structure that in other ways had been strengthened by the 1973 consent decree.

The Impact of Technological Change on the Work Process

Before examining the changes in personnel policies that resulted from the aforementioned transformations, it is helpful to take a closer look at the changes in the work process brought about by the introduction of computer-based switching technology in the early 1970s.

Electronic Switching

The nerve center of the telephone system is the central office where switches are located. Switches route telephone traffic through the network.

The first electronic switching system (ESS) was introduced by AT&T in 1965. At New York Telephone, the massive phase-in of first-generation ESSs began in the late 1960s. By the early 1980s, only a few upstate switches remained to be rebuilt with electronic switches.[2]

The earlier electromechanical switches (panel and cross bar systems) needed considerable routine maintenance. In large central offices, the telephone company employed on a daily basis upward of 30 or 40 technicians to maintain and repair switches (*Business Week*, March 24, 1980). The job of switchman entailed electrical and mechanical skills for repair as well as analytic skills for diagnosis.

Electronic switching uses microelectronic circuitry and computer technology to direct telephone traffic. The most advanced ESS available today, ESS-5, can route about 550,000 calls an hour, four times as many calls as could be handled by the most advanced electromechanical units. In addition, a great deal of the capacity for troubleshooting is engineered into the electronic switching equipment itself, so the number of switchmen needed in central offices is much lower than in the past. With the most recent generation of ESSs, two or three switchmen are often sufficient; in some instances, central offices do not even have an in-house switchman (Newman, 1981).

The introduction of electronic switching made possible not only a sizable reduction in the number of switchmen needed to maintain the new equipment but also a dramatic reorganization in the way maintenance is organized. Many of the functions associated with maintenance are now centralized in automated switching control centers (ASCC) (Howard, 1980). ASCCs serve as control rooms linked electronically to several central offices from which traffic flows and breakdowns in the switches can be monitored continuously. ASCCs are manned on a twenty-four-hour basis by traffic technicians and switchmen who spot troubles and put switches out of service when needed. The information is then relayed to switchmen located at the central offices who move in and repair or replace the faulty circuits.

Another way in which the tasks of switchmen changed is in the repair of trunk lines. In the past, switchmen located in the central offices were also responsible for diagnosing trunk-line difficulties. They would locate the defective trunk and take it out of service until the problem had been analyzed and repaired. Today, as in the case of the switchmen, one or two technicians are in charge of monitoring trunk lines remotely from the ASCCs. Breakdowns are first handled by the ASCC technicians who then dispatch someone else to proceed with the repair (Howard, 1980).

In short, the introduction of electronic switching has substantially reorganized the way maintenance is handled, involving perhaps a sharper distinction between tasks performed in the control centers and those performed in the field. Maintenance tasks associated with ESSs continue to require substantial skills, although of a different nature than those required by the old electromechanical switches. The tasks might involve, for example, the editing of computer programs stored in the system. Some of these tasks, however, have become the responsibility of management engineers, where in the past equivalent tasks would have been largely handled by the switchmen themselves. This transfer of responsibility has been a major point of contention between switchmen and management, with the former arguing that part of their jobs and skills has been taken away from them.

The other area most directly affected by the introduction of electronic switching has been operator service. In the traffic service position system (TSPS) offices, old cord boards have been replaced with computer consoles. Today, operator assistance requires pushing buttons, which is much faster and less demanding physically than the plugs of the old switchboards. In addition, today's TSPS terminals handle electronically all of the tasks associated with timing calls, calculating tolls, and performing record-keeping operations, all of which were once performed manually by operators. As a result, the new technology has sent productivity soaring from an average of 20 phone calls per hour per operator with the old cord board to today's 100 calls per hour (i.e., an average of 35 seconds spent answering a call). These major changes have taken place at the same time that electronic switching technology has enabled increased numbers of calls to be dialed directly. Operators are now employed primarily for international calls and directory assistance. All together, these changes explain the dramatic decrease in the number of operators needed to run the system (Howard, 1980).

Other Technological Changes

While clearly some of the most dramatic technological changes have occurred in central offices and operator offices, other areas have been affected by the new technology. To a large extent, technological change has been pervasive throughout the entire business.

In the outside craft departments, the move toward universal installation of jack-compatible connecting boxes on customer premises and the computerization of the network have reduced dramatically the number of installers needed to serve customer premises. Customers are now able to move from one location to another carrying along their own equipment and, in some areas, keeping their original telephone number. As long as the customer remains within the perimeter of the same central office, the telephone company can simply program the relocation of the particular telephone number into its switchboard.

Finally, in supporting areas such as billing and accounting, computerization has also been extensive.

The Transformation of New York Telephone's Personnel Organization Under the 1973–1979 AT&T-EEO-C Consent Decree

New York Telephone's Personnel Organization
Before the 1970s

In the heyday of the AT&T monopoly, New York Telephone, like other Bell subsidiaries, was an engineering-oriented organization. The key departments were the inside and outside craft departments, the operator service department, and the customer service department.

In terms of personnel, departments operated independently. Each department hired its own people for entry-level positions: framemen in switches, linemen in network, telephone operators in operator services, and so forth. Training was organized on a departmental basis, with supervisors doing much of it on the job. With seniority, experience, and on-the-job training, rank-and-file employees could expect to reach middle-management, if not upper-management, positions. During periods of in-house shortages, departments would recruit some skilled employees or entry-level executives directly from the external labor market, but such recruiting tended to be exceptional.

While successful in providing opportunities for upward mobility, this system had many flaws. For all practical purposes, departments were strongly "sex and race labeled." The craft departments, which offered the best-paying positions and the best-laddered opportunities, were mostly restricted to white males. Females were confined to operator service, customer service, or certain supporting departments, which did not pay as well and which, comparatively speaking, offered fewer opportunities for upward mobility. Blacks and other minorities tended to be segregated in even lower paying occupations in supporting areas such as janitorial services and building maintenance.

The major business and technological developments of the early 1970s forced many changes in this system. The system of mobility ladders had to be altered drastically among nonexempt workers to permit the following:

1. Sizable shifts of people out of areas in which employment needed to be reduced, especially out of operator service.
2. Rapid staff buildup in areas such as marketing, business service, residence service, corporate development (planning, personnel, etc.),

and finance, which were expanding as the company responded to changes in its market environment.

3. Major adjustments in the sex and race composition of the company's occupational mix in response to the 1973 AT&T-EEO-C consent decree.

Among executives, the pressures were mostly to fulfill two needs:

1. The need for employment growth in staff (technical) as opposed to line (supervisory) positions in areas as diverse as engineering, sales, and marketing as the company responded to both market and technological changes.
2. The need for a less discriminatory occupational sex-race mix for nonexempt workers.

The 1973 Upgrade and Transfer Plan
for Nonexempt Workers

The first Upgrade and Transfer Plan (UTP) was introduced in the early 1970s as a way to move surplus employees from declining to growing occupations. A principal target of the plan was to shift large numbers of women from the operator service departments to the residence and business customer service departments. With the advent of the consent decree in 1973, the original UTP was formalized, becoming part of the agreement worked out between EEO-C and the company. The plan was altered, however, so that it could be used to promote adjustments in the sex and race composition of the company's major classes of jobs, for example, by building female and minority employment in craft occupations while bringing white-male employees into operator and customer service positions.

In its simplest formulation, the 1973 UTP worked as follows (Northrup and Larson, 1979):

1. The UTP opened *lateral ladders*, that is, opportunities for employees in one department to move to a job in another department, regardless of prior job experience and departmental affiliation.
2. The company committed itself to filling most job openings (other than low-skilled entry-level positions) through in-house promotions (lateral or upward) rather than by resorting to hiring in the external labor market.
3. Job openings and applications for openings were centralized under the control of a single personnel department. Qualification was now defined on the basis of a general aptitude test which did not

TABLE 4.3
New York Telephone Job Classifications

Job Classes	Job Description
Management	
1	Upper-level management.
2	Middle-level management.
3	Entry-level management.
4	Administrative positions such as senior secretaries and supervisors. Also included are advanced data processors.
Nonmanagement	
5	Nonmanagerial sales workers. Included are communications consultants, commercial representatives, and directory advertising salesmen.
6	Skilled outside craft workers such as PBX installers and repairmen.
7	Skilled inside craft workers such as switchmen.
8	Skilled general-service employees including draftsmen, mechanics, and drivers.
9	Entry-level outside craft workers, primarily linemen.
10	Entry-level inside craft workers such as framemen.
11	Skilled clerical workers such as senior clerks, computer attendants, and service representatives.
12	Semiskilled clerical workers including stenographers and administrative clerks.
13	Entry-level clerical positions including typists and routing clerks.
14	Telephone operators.
15	Entry-level service workers such as cooks, elevator operators, and building maintenance.

Source: New York Telephone Company data; *Equal Opportunity in New York Telephone, Employee's Guide,* 1973.

account for prior, skill-related experience. Pools of applicants were divided between "qualified" and "qualified plus," with the latter differing from the former on the basis of seniority.

4. The UTP introduced a provision permitting qualified female and minority employees to override white males otherwise more qualified on the basis of departmental seniority (qualified plus).

5. The UTP called for meeting sex and race targets in 15 major job classes (see Table 4.3) specified on the basis of the sex and race composition of local labor markets and the company's standing in 1973. Where needed, targets were to be met by using the

override provision to select employees from the pool of qualified and qualified plus applicants.

Overall adjustments in the promotional structure were considerable. In 1970 New York Telephone hired 35,000 nonexempt employees, while close to 30,000 left the company. Had such high turnover continued, the company would have had considerable flexibility in meeting sex and race targets by hiring women and minorities from the external labor market to fill specific underrepresented positions. But by 1974, because of the company's need to reduce overall employment, its commitment to promote from within and its emphasis on stronger employee attachment to improve the quality of service, New York Telephone hired only 101 new nonexempt employees from the external labor market. All in-house openings were filled through in-house promotion, with a high premium placed on finding qualified women and minorities employed by the company to move into many of these openings. The company had no choice but to use the override provision extensively.

Women and minority workers who had previously been denied access to craft departments became framemen, switchmen, linesmen, and installers (see Table 4.3), while openings were created for white men in the operator service and commercial departments. Not surprisingly, the unions, which had traditionally represented white men in craft departments, strongly opposed the override clause. They challenged it in court, but the court upheld the consent decree, and the unions were forced to accept the provision. Later, as a way to weaken the distinction between qualified and qualified plus workers, AT&T broadened the concept of seniority, interpreted originally as departmental seniority, by extending it to mean length of service within the entire Bell system and regardless of departmental affiliation. While data for New York Telephone alone are not available, evidence of the importance of the override clause in filling job openings at AT&T during the first few years of the decree is presented in Table 4.4. The data show that during the period of 1973 to 1974, 25 percent of AT&T openings in job classes 5 through 12 were filled through override, with seniority then strictly defined as departmental tenure. During 1975 to 1976, with the broader definition of companywide tenure, the equivalent statistics hovered around 10 to 13 percent.

Internal Ladders for Executives

As in the case of nonexempt employees, mobility among executives had to be altered in order to open to women and minorities the positions

TABLE 4.4
AT&T: Use of the Affirmative Action Override, 1973–1976

	1973–1974[a]	1975[b]	1976[b]
Total Openings in Job Classes 5–12	112,819	33,982	20,593
Total Use of the Override	28,856	4,529	2,094
Overrides as a Percentage of Total Openings	25.6	13.3	10.2

Note: Data for New York Telephone alone are not available.
[a] Seniority defined in terms of departmental tenure.
[b] Seniority defined in terms of companywide tenure.
Source: Herbert R. Northrup and John A. Larson, *The Impact of the AT&T-EEO Consent Decree,* Labor Relations and Public Policy Series, vol. 20 (Philadelphia: University of Pennsylvania, 1979).

in which they had long been underrepresented. As with the UTP, specific targets were set for each major managerial job class and subclass.[3]

Meanwhile, the shift to stronger marketing, the growing importance of engineering- and computer-related functions associated with the introduction of new technology, and the development of supporting functions such as finance, legal counsel, and others forced the company to place greater emphasis on hiring and promoting staff rather than line managers. Departments such as marketing, business services, business sales, and personnel began competing with the traditional departments (technical services) for attention, resources, and personnel.

In a broad sense, the shift from line to staff managers contributed importantly to deemphasizing the in-house mobility of rank-and-file employees with limited formal education while stressing the direct recruiting of better-prepared, college-educated personnel in the external labor market.

While the company did not make available data showing the employee breakdown between in-house promotions and external recruits among first-level management personnel, in-depth probing of personnel officials suggests that by the mid–1970s in-house promotion had become relatively insignificant. In contrast, the same officials observed that many of the older managers who had entered managerial ranks from within earlier (in the 1950s and 1960s) lacked a college education.

In the absence of data on the shift from in-house to external hiring of managerial personnel, the breakdown of New York Telephone's college

TABLE 4.5
New York Telephone: First-Level Management College Recruits, 1981

	All Sexes and Races	Female and Minorities
Total	275	102
Sales	167	57
Associate Account Executives and Communications System Representatives		
General Management	108	45
Supervisors and Administrators		
Engineers, Programmers, and Systems Analysts		
Fast-track Managers (see text)		

Source: New York Telephone Company data.

graduate recruits provided by the company is at least indicative of the shift from line to staff personnel. In 1981 New York Telephone recruited 275 entry-level managers on college campuses. The breakdowns are shown in Table 4.5.

Almost two-thirds of the new recruits were hired in sales. Most were expected to join a marketing team of three to four people with responsibility for a particular geographic and functional area (e.g., small banks in the Buffalo area). About one-fourth of the new sales recruits came in with a business administration or marketing background to head the sales teams as associate account executives; the other three-fourths had a technical background, typically an engineering degree, and became communications system representatives on a sales team.

The remaining one-third of all new recruits came in under the general-management classification. Most were college graduates with an engineering or a computer science background hired for technical positions in craft departments. A few were recruited as supervisors and administrators to staff traditional first- or second-level supervisory positions. A small, last group was recruited to join a fast track, called the *management career development track*, whose purpose was to prepare administrators for upper-echelon positions. In 1981, 42 of the new hires from the general-management classification, including 18 females and minorities, were placed in this fast track. As a rule, these employees were required to reach second-level management positions within two years at the latest. At a minimum, they had a four-year college education, had graduated in the top one-third of their class (or with a B+ average), and had some work experience.

The Implications of Organizational and Technological Changes for Employment Opportunities in the Early and Mid-1970s

In short, by the early and mid–1970s employment opportunities at New York Telephone had begun to change profoundly. In this section, changes are highlighted along five dimensions: (1) job openings, (2) hiring practices and educational barriers, (3) training and skills, (4) sex and race barriers, and (5) earnings.

Job Openings

Detailed employment data describing the shift that occurred at New York Telephone as a result of the changes analyzed earlier were not made available by the company. In *The Impact of the AT&T-EEO Consent Decree*, however, Northrup and Larson (1979) present data for AT&T's Mid-Atlantic region for 1973 and 1979 (see Table 4.6). The region combines employment at New York Telephone, New Jersey Telephone, and Bell of Pennsylvania, roughly in the ratios of 60, 20, and 20 percent (see Table 4.7).

To a large extent, changes that occurred in the Mid-Atlantic region during the 1973–1979 period were similar to those presented earlier in this chapter for the whole of AT&T (see Table 4.2; also last column in Table 4.6). In relative terms, the 1970s saw the buildup of sales personnel and officials and managers, while there was attrition among operators and service workers and stagnation among craft and clerical workers. The Mid-Atlantic region experienced a net employment decline during the 1973–1979 period, while the AT&T overall employment level remained roughly the same, suggesting that overall employment at AT&T is in part correlated to the size of the consumer base. Hence, in fast-growing regions, local companies were able to offset contraction resulting from technologically induced productivity gains with some growth attributable to expanding demand. Operating subsidiaries in declining regions, however, typically lacked this equilibrating mechanism.

Table 4.7 underscores the productivity gains brought about at New York Telephone by the introduction of new technology during the 1970s. Measured in constant 1967 dollars, operating revenues per employee more than doubled between 1970 and 1979, from $18,513 to $39,072. The table also shows considerable flattening of this productivity trend during the late 1970s and the early 1980s, a phenomenon reflecting in

TABLE 4.6
AT&T Labor Force in the Mid-Atlantic Region: Numbers and Percentage Shares
of Employees, 1973–1979

	Numbers		% Shares		Mid-Atlantic Region % Change from	AT&T All Regions % Change from
	1979	1973	1979	1973	1973–1979	1973–1979[a]
Officials & Managers	32,530	30,988	23.9	20.2	5.0	16.4
Administrative	6,842	8,860	5.0	5.8	−22.8	12.5
Sales Workers	1,130	933	0.8	0.6	21.1	27.9
Clerical	37,478	39,333	27.5	25.6	−4.7	11.4
Operators	14,964	23,680	11.0	15.4	−36.8	−28.7
Outside Crafts	24,513	27,824	18.0	18.1	−11.9	−1.0
Inside Crafts	16,533	16,214	12.1	10.6	2.0	0.4
Service Workers	2,085	5,840	1.5	3.8	−64.0	−53.8
Total	136,075	153,672	100.0	100.0	−11.5	0.2

Note: Officials & Managers include Job Classes 1, 2, 3; Administrative, Job Class 4; Sales Workers, Job Class 5; Clerical, Job Classes 11, 12, 13; Operators, Job Class 14; Outside Crafts, Job Classes 6, 9; Inside Crafts, Job Classes 7, 10; Service Workers, Job Classes 8, 15. See Table 4.3.
[a] From Table 4.2.
Source: AT&T, *EEO-1 Reports,* 1973 and 1979; Herbert R. Northrup and John A. Larson, *The Impact of the AT&T-EEO Consent Decree,* Labor Relations and Public Policy Series, vol. 20 (Philadelphia: University of Pennsylvania, 1979).

part some of the labor problems that arose in response to the introduction of the new technology. These problems are discussed further in the last section of this chapter.

Hiring Practices, Educational Barriers to Entry, and Mobility Opportunities

As indicated earlier, the 1970s brought about major changes in hiring practices. To recall, whereas departments once did their own hiring and training, the introduction of UTP led to a companywide centralization of both functions.

As a result of the consent decree, all semiskilled and skilled positions in craft departments were closed to outside hire. This came about because of the need to bring women and minorities already employed by the

TABLE 4.7
New York Telephone: Total Employment, Total Operating Revenues, and Operating
Revenues per Employee, 1970–1981

	Employment			Operating Revenues, NY Tel (billions of $)	$ of Operating Revenues per Employee, NY Telephone	
	NY Tel	NJ Tel	Bell of PA		Current $	1967 $[a]
1970	103,000			2.048	19,883	18,513
1973	89,500	32,265	34,330	2.843	31,765	25,596
1976	80,000			3.885	48,503	33,358
1979	78,000	29,000	32,000	4.861	62,320	39,072
1981	81,000			5.944	73,338	40,518

[a] Using consumer price index deflator for other utilities and public services.

Source: Moody's Public Utility Manuals (New York: Moody's Investors Service,
several years).

company into these better departments or into better positions through
lateral and upward transfers. Consequently, under the 1973–1979 UTP,
new recruits were brought into the company exclusively as operators,
clerks, or service workers (job classes 13, 14, and 15). Once hired, new
employees were asked to stay in these entry positions for a minimum
of one year before requesting an interdepartmental transfer or intra-
departmental promotion. With the UTP, the company found it increasingly
difficult to hire workers with previous training (i.e., students from
vocational schools or experienced workers); many were reluctant to take
a low-skilled job before being entitled to apply for a semiskilled or
skilled position.

For a time at least, this development led to a great deal of uniformity
in hiring standards for nonexempt employees, with the company focusing
on high school graduates or the equivalent. It is useful to recall here
that nonexempt hiring was extremely limited during most of the 1970s.
In 1974, for example, only 101 such employees were hired in nonexempt
positions.

Among exempt personnel, hiring, as noted earlier, shifted sharply
from internal promotion to outside hiring, with four-year college diplomas
becoming prerequisites to employment in managerial ranks. In effect,
by the mid–1970s New York Telephone had created a two-tier hiring
system, with almost complete elimination of the ladders of mobility
from nonexempt to exempt ranks.

Training and Skills

The 1970s saw a dramatic surge in company-sponsored training at New York Telephone. This occurred because of: (1) the changing nature of the technology and the widespread need for retraining; (2) the increasing need for training directly associated with the multiplication of lateral and upward shifts of workers under the UTP; and (3) the lowering of hiring requirements for all nonexempt recruits to high school diplomas, often resulting in yet additional training needs.

Beginning in 1971, all training was centralized in the Human Resource Development Division. In 1981, when nearly 68,000 employees received some form of company training, New York Telephone estimated that it spent nearly $150 million on training—including salaries of instructors, costs of instruction, and salaries of nonexempt workers who needed to be replaced during training. As of 1982, the Human Resource Development Division employed 585 full-time employees—instructors, course developers, supervisors, and support people—and operated from five main locations—two in New York City and one each in Long Island, Albany, and northwest New York State.

Training provided by the division focused on five major areas: computers (for programmers and systems analysts), engineering, maintenance crafts,[4] management (especially sales and business office), and generic training (skill development, supervisory skills).

Training at the entry level was typically simple and of short duration. As soon as employees moved into semiskilled and skilled positions, however, many required ongoing training largely because of the continuous upgrading of the technology. In outside crafts, for example, installers had to be trained regularly to handle new pieces of equipment. Likewise, service representatives in the commercial departments had to be familiarized with new systems made available to customers (basic training for "service reps" lasts 13 weeks).

While most technical training tended to be offered in house (as noted later, this is now changing), a good deal of the management and generic training programs offered in the 1970s emphasized reliance on outside training resources. By the late 1970s, such programs included a career skill program, a tuition aid program, a management career-development program, and an executive development program. The career skill program was aimed at nonmanagement personnel with deficient schooling and needing upgrading before becoming eligible for transfer. It was basically a three R's remedial program taught at SUNY, CUNY, and several community colleges, with New York Telephone paying most of the tuition. According to human resource officials, attendance tended to be heavily minority, with typically several hundred employees registered in the program at any one time.

The tuition aid program was for employees seeking a college education. Typically, it was sought by noncollege-educated upper-echelon nonexempt employees hoping to become lower-echelon managers. Employees were allowed to register in a four-year-college program as long as it was work related,[5] and the company picked up part of the tuition. On the whole, according to human resource officials, very few took advantage of the program.

The management career-development program—the fast-track management program—was conducted mostly in house and placed a heavy emphasis on business management training.

Finally, New York Telephone sponsored special programs for managers. In particular, New York Telephone sent some of its first- and second-level managers to Columbia University's evening and weekend two-year master of business administration program and some of its high-level executives to Columbia University's executive development program at Arden House.

By the mid-1980s, while there was a continuing need for in-house training for both exempt and nonexempt employees, especially in firm-specific skills (e.g., familiarization with new equipment), the company came under new pressure to make much greater use of external resources than it had up until that point. This meant contracting out a greater number of training programs or avoiding altogether the need for company-sponsored instruction by hiring trained personnel when needed. Indeed, a principal change in UTP after 1979 was a return to recruiting skilled technical personnel in the external labor market—a point to which I return below.

Sex and Race Barriers

How successful was the introduction of the UTP in altering the sex and race composition of employment at New York Telephone? Here again, detailed data were not made available by New York Telephone, but data from Northrup and Larson (1979) on AT&T's Mid-Atlantic region shed some light on what went on.

Table 4.8 breaks down the occupational distribution of the labor force for 1973 and 1979 by major group, including white males, white females, minority males, and minority females, and shows the relative gains and losses of these groups in each occupation over the 1973–1979 period.

The data reveal that despite clear advances the company continued to be characterized by considerable occupational segregation as of 1979. In 1973 over 95 percent of the clerical employees and 97 percent of the operators were either white females or minorities. In the craft departments, over 90 percent of outside craft employees and close to

TABLE 4.8
Occupational Distribution of Major Groups of Workers: AT&T Mid-Atlantic Region, 1979 and 1973 (in percentages)

	1979					1973				
	Occupation as % of All Labor Force	Major Sex-Race Group as % Employment in Occupation[a]				Occupation as % of All Labor Force	Major Sex-Race Group as % Employment in Occupation[a]			
		White Male	White Female	Minority Male	Minority Female		White Male	White Female	Minority Male	Minority Female
Officials & Managers	23.9	72.0	21.1	3.5	3.4	20.2	78.4	18.2	1.8	1.6
Administrative	5.0	10.8	66.1	2.2	20.9	5.8	7.3	77.0	1.2	14.5
Sales Workers	0.8	51.2	28.9	10.0	9.9	0.6	47.5	38.1	5.2	9.2
Clerical	27.5	7.9	61.0	2.6	28.5	25.6	4.6	69.0	2.1	22.3
Telephone Operators	11.1	3.9	61.6	1.0	33.5	15.4	2.7	63.7	0.6	33.0
Outside Crafts	18.0	89.6	1.0	9.2	0.2	18.1	90.7	0.2	9.1	0.0
Inside Crafts	12.1	79.0	7.2	11.6	2.3	10.6	84.4	3.3	11.5	0.8
Service Workers	1.5	38.6	26.0	26.0	9.5	3.8	56.2	15.4	23.9	4.4
All Occupations	100.0	47.1	33.6	5.3	14.0	100.0	45.2	36.8	4.9	12.8

[a] Each line adds to 100 percent.

Occupational Overrepresentation or Underrepresentation of Major Groups of Workers: 1979 and 1973

	1979				1973			
	White Male	White Female	Minority Male	Minority Female	White Male	White Female	Minority Male	Minority Female
Officials & Managers	1.53	0.63	0.66	0.24	1.73	0.49	0.37	0.13
Administrative	0.23	1.97	0.42	1.49	0.16	2.09	0.24	1.13
Sales Workers	1.09	0.86	1.89	0.71	1.05	1.04	1.06	0.72
Clerical	0.17	1.82	0.49	2.04	0.10	1.88	0.43	1.74
Telephone Operators	0.08	1.83	0.19	2.39	0.06	1.73	0.12	2.58
Outside Crafts	1.90	0.03	1.74	0.02	2.01	0.01	1.86	0.00
Inside Crafts	1.68	0.21	2.19	0.16	1.87	0.09	2.35	0.06
Service Workers	0.82	0.77	4.90	0.68	1.24	0.42	4.88	0.34

Note: The five principal occupations are underlined for emphasis. The index of representation is measured as the ratio of the share of employment of a major group in a given occupation divided by its share of all employment. A ratio above 1 indicates overrepresentation; below 1, underrepresentation.

Source: AT&T, *EEO-1 Reports*, 1973 and 1979; Herbert R. Northrup and John A. Larson, *The Impact of the AT&T-EEO Consent Decree*, Labor Relations and Public Policy Series, vol. 20 (Philadelphia: University of Pennsylvania, 1979).

TABLE 4.9
Occupational Distribution of Major Groups of Workers: New York Telephone, 1982, Compared to AT&T Mid-Atlantic Region, 1979

	New York Telephone, 1982			AT&T Mid-Atlantic Region, 1979		
	Males	Females	Minorities[a]	Males	Females	Minorities[a]
Management[b]	60.8	39.2	15.2	64.6	35.4	9.7
Nonmanagement	46.2	53.8	30.7	47.5	52.5	23.2
All Occupations	50.3	49.7	26.3	52.4	47.6	19.3

[a] Includes male and female minorities.
[b] Includes categories of officials and managers and administrative (see Table 4.3).

Sources: New York Telephone company data; Herbert R. Northrup and John A. Larson, *The Impact of the AT&T-EEO Consent Decree*, Labor Relations and Public Policy Series, vol. 20 (Philadelphia: University of Pennsylvania, 1979).

85 percent of inside craft employees were white males. Only minority males had secured a solid access to these positions. Within management, white and minority females accounted for most of the administrative employees, but these jobs tended to be deadend, front-line supervisory positions. Over three-fourths of the officials and managers were white males.

By 1979 marked advances had been recorded in three of the five principal occupational groups: Among officials and managers, white women, minority men, and minority women had increased their shares substantially; among clerical workers, large shares of white men and minority women had been brought in; and among inside crafts, white women, in particular, had improved their share markedly. By comparison, among operators and outside crafts, the impact of occupational desegregation remained very slim, although these were the two most segregated occupational groups to begin with. On the whole, much remained to be done.

Table 4.9 presents limited data comparing New York Telephone in 1982 to AT&T's Mid-Atlantic region in 1979. Assuming that New York Telephone's 1979 employment distribution did not differ substantially from that of AT&T's Mid-Atlantic region, the data suggest continued improvement in the most recent period, at least in bringing larger shares of white women and minority workers into managerial ranks.

TABLE 4.10
Average Weekly Earnings of Production and Nonsupervisory Workers in Total
Private Industry and in Transportation and Public Utilities (in current dollars)

	Total Private Industry (1)	Transportation and Public Utilities (2)	Ratio (2):(1) (3)
1968	107.73	138.85	1.29
1970	119.46	155.93	1.30
1973	145.43	204.62	1.41
1976	175.45	257.75	1.47
1979	219.30	326.38	1.49
1982	255.19	391.02	1.53

Source: Monthly Labor Review, several years.

Earnings

In the absence of a specific earnings series for New York Telephone, Table 4.10, based on several issues of *Monthly Labor Review*, shows the evolution of average weekly earnings of nonexempt employees in the transportation and public utilities industry group for the period 1968 to 1982. The table suggests that until 1982 there were markedly higher average earnings for these industries than for total private industry and, for that matter, a growing differential between the two.

New York Telephone Personnel Organization in the Post–Consent Decree Era: Implications for Employment Opportunities

The End of the AT&T-EEO-C Consent Decree

For the record, it is useful to note here that two years into the implementation of the consent decree (1975) AT&T was found lagging in meeting EEO objectives. Major midcourse adjustments had to be made. By 1979, EEO-C found the company in sufficient fulfillment of the decree's requirements to allow it to lapse. AT&T and New York Telephone decided to continue on with the UTP but with one major change—the dropping of the override clause.

In part, the override clause was eliminated to diffuse the resentment of the unions. However, the company remained accountable for improving sex and race composition among its semiskilled and skilled labor force.

In effect, this brought the company back into the external labor market where it could hire trained female and minority workers for semiskilled and skilled positions. In short, it reopened middle-level entry to outside recruits and, by default, weakened the high level of internal mobility that had been achieved under the 1973 decree.

Union opposition to the override clause was obviously not the single reason for change. Looming large was growing competition from other telecommunications carriers and the resulting pressure on AT&T and its subsidiaries for labor cost containment. The system that had evolved at AT&T under the 1973–1979 UTP was extremely costly since it required that the company shoulder enormous training costs. Meanwhile, competitors were hiring skilled workers away from AT&T and hiring trained recruits directly from vocational schools and community colleges. In short, competitors were busy finding ways to minimize their direct investment in human resources.

1982: The Dawn of a New Era

On January 8, 1982, AT&T entered into a consent decree with the U.S. Justice Department by which it settled a seven-year-old court case brought about by the department. The charge was that Ma Bell had abused its monopoly by consistently taking steps to keep competitors out of the market for equipment and long distance phone service. The heart of the settlement required that AT&T divest itself of all its local operating subsidiaries, reducing AT&T primarily to a long distance service provider and a manufacturer and marketer of telephone equipment. In return, the new AT&T was also allowed to enter previously excluded fields, namely, computer hardware and software. The company had long produced computer hardware and software for its own needs but was not allowed to sell its computer products (*New York Times*, 1982).

On January 1, 1984, the old AT&T was dismantled. From a labor market point of view, the company breakup completed a process of demand fragmentation which had been building since the late 1970s with the emergence of the new long-distance service providers as serious competitors. The result was a further push by all competitors to externalize the process of skill formation. In an attempt to bring some order into the marketplace, shortly after AT&T's divestiture a number of the largest carriers, including some of the newly independent operating companies and several of the new long distance carriers (MCI, Sprint, and others), created the National Telecommunications Education Council. The purpose of the council is to finance the development of training curricula in community and four-year colleges to prepare semiskilled and skilled employees for the industry. In the New York area, Brooklyn Polytechnic

Institute and several of the four-year colleges and community colleges have become involved in that effort (Freedman, 1984).

One additional manpower development is worthy of note because it is indicative of further loosening of the employment arrangements of the past. Even prior to the dismantling of the old AT&T, New York Telephone had broken a basic rule of the company and had begun hiring part-time employees in the phone center stores which it was opening to market residential equipment. While numerically small (in 1982 New York Telephone estimated that only 2 percent of its labor force was employed part-time), this new employee group demonstrated the company's willingness to reform to meet a changing business environment.

In concluding this review of New York Telephone's evolving personnel organization, it seems reasonable to argue that the strengthening of the system of internal labor markets under the EEO-C consent decree was a short-lived development. In effect, this temporary strengthening went against forces pulling in the opposite direction—forces that ultimately would prevail.

Notes

1. Until the late 1960s, welfare recipients were not allowed telephone service. This rule was overturned, and a large number began asking for telephones at a time when the number of families on the welfare rolls reached a peak in New York City.

2. Note that electronic switching technology has changed over the years. The first generation of ESSs was based on switching "analog" signals. The most recent generation (ESS–5) switches "digital" signals, and necessitates that analog voice messages be converted into digital messages. This technology makes computer data transfer through the telephone network more efficient than earlier. Today, this most advanced switching technology is in place only in a limited number of central offices, primarily in the borough of Manhattan (New York City).

3. The four management job classes shown in Table 4.3 are organized into eight management levels. In turn, management positions are organized around functional groups, functional areas, departments, and districts, giving rise to many job subclasses.

4. Technical courses often were developed through cooperative arrangements with other companies in the Bell system.

5. *Work related* was loosely defined: anything within liberal arts, business, law, or engineering, but not, for example, within medicine.

5

Finance: The Case of
a Large Insurance Firm

For many years, employment and output in the insurance industry (including carriers, agencies, and brokers) grew at a healthy pace, frequently outperforming the rest of the economy (see Table 5.1). Today, however, the sense throughout the industry is that employment trends have lost their momentum. Between 1980 and 1984, the industry added a mere 100,000 jobs nationwide, a far cry from what could have been expected in the wake of the 400,000 jobs added by the industry during the 1970s (see Table 5.2). This downturn looked even more dramatic once it was observed that recent employment growth had occurred mostly in agencies and brokers' offices, suggesting continued employment growth in product delivery and servicing but sharp declines in product processing.

This chapter explains this process of transformation, identifies its origins, and assesses its impact on employment opportunities by means of a case study of one large life insurance carrier.

The 1970s: A Decade of Traumatic Changes
for the Insurance Industry

By most accounts, insurers entered the 1970s unaware of the extent to which their industry would be forced to change during the decade. In every respect, the 1960s had been very good years for the industry. The general tendency toward expanded coverage of many kinds of risks, partly under the impulse of the Great Society programs, had brought solid growth in areas of commercial risk coverage, group medical insurance, workers' compensation, and pension fund management. Indeed, opportunities were so good that in life insurance alone the number of carriers grew from 650 in 1950 to 1,750 in 1979 (*Wall Street Journal*, 1983). In an environment characterized by heavy regulation and low inflation, the insurance industry was virtually guaranteed access to large cash flows that could be used to generate large investment income at low cost.

By the early 1970s, however, the industry found itself caught in a web of change—including high inflation and high interest rates, deregulation, intensifying competition, and new technology—which would transform radically the economics of the business. Of all of these factors, inflation might have ultimately caused the most disruption. Reacting to inflation, carriers raised premiums. By mid-decade, interest rates moved into the two-digit range, while returns on policies were kept artificially low—often as low as 3 or 4 percent.

Consumer reaction to these trends was predictable. Retail consumers of property-casualty insurance pressured state regulators to cap premium increases on personal-line products, especially automobile coverage. In commercial lines, large corporate customers circumvented insurers by purchasing actuarial underwriting services from insurers and setting up so-called *captive* insurance firms in which the funds needed to cover risks were pooled. This approach allowed corporate customers to retain both the management of their funds and the returns on such funds. In life insurance, the industry was plagued by a sizable cash outflow during the 1970s when consumers borrowed against their policies at low rates in order to reinvest the funds profitably elsewhere.

The reaction of insurers to the defensive moves of consumers was threefold: (1) development of new products to compete with those of other financial institutions, (2) price competition, and (3) cost control. The rolling out of new insurance products would not have been possible were it not for a simultaneous process of deregulation which many of the largest insurers pushed for during the 1970s. In life insurance, for example, Equitable introduced the first variable life insurance product in 1976, which the company dubbed "life insurance for people that are investors at heart" (*Wall Street Journal*, 1983). With variable life insurance, death benefits are guaranteed. The cash value buildup of the policy, however, varies, depending on the performance of a separate account invested in stocks, bonds, or money market securities. While only Prudential and Metropolitan followed suit, Equitable's variable life insurance opened the way for universal life insurance, a product introduced in 1979 by E. F. Hutton Life and marketed by over 100 insurers by 1982. Generally speaking, universal life is considered less risky than variable life. Finally, in keeping with the continued blurring of lines between various financial institutions, by the early 1980s some life insurers were also offering brokerage services and marketing IRAs, KEOGHs, money funds, and other savings products.

regionalizing several of its major product divisions by decentralizing staff and facilities.

Divisions that employed large numbers of clericals—individual life, group life and group medical, pensions, and real estate—became the principal targets of the regionalization effect. Processing work traditionally carried out in the home office—policy rating, document preparation, claim processing, premium calculation, billing, and other functions— was decentralized to regional processing centers.

In effect, the regionalization program involved not only decentralizing the processing functions formerly carried out in the home office but also regrouping preprocessing, mailing, and other activities traditionally handled at the district level. In individual life, for example, the company once maintained general-service offices to prepare forms to be sent to the home office and, generally speaking, to interface with customers. Bills and checks, for example, used to be prepared at the home office but were mailed by agents via the local general-service offices. The company maintained roughly one such office per sales district (approximately 90 general-service offices for 125 sales districts). In the end, however, these offices tended to be small, and the great majority of the processing clerks were employed in the home office.

In group medical insurance, where contracts often cover thousands of employees of a single corporate client, the company used to maintain field offices that handled a portion of the processing associated with claims. This was done partly as a way to maintain a personalized relationship with customers and partly because of the frequent need for claim adjusters to deal directly with a client's benefits officer. At one point, the company had up to 97 such field offices. Compared to life insurance products, a fairly substantial share of processing clerks in group medical were employed in these field offices.

In short then, in individual life and in group life, the emphasis of the regionalization effort was mostly on decentralizing work away from the home office. The company retained a six-region concept, opening regional processing centers for individual life in Fresno, Des Moines, Charlotte, Columbus, Colorado Springs, and Milford (Conn.). (The regional processing center for the northeast area in group life was located on Long Island, N.Y., rather than in Milford, Conn.) By comparison, in group medical, where the labor force had traditionally been far more decentralized in the field offices, the focus was on merging local offices. By the early 1980s, the number of field offices had been cut roughly by half, down to 45 from the original 97, with a long-range target of approximately 10 to 12 processing centers. This process was expected to take longer to carry out because of the disruption associated with

TABLE 5.3
Distribution of Employees at the Insurance Company: Home and Field Offices,
1971–1983

	1971		1975		1980		1983	
	#	%	#	%	#	%	#	%
Home	7,418	59.0	6,998	50.0	6,049	36.0	5,473	37.0
Field	5,225	41.0	6,986	50.0	10,621	64.0	9,348	63.0
Total	12,643	100.0	13,984	100.0	16,660	100.0	14,821	100.0

Source: Insurance Company data.

the closing of field offices in which large numbers of people might have
once been employed.

The effect of the regionalization program on the company's labor
force is shown in Table 5.3. By 1980 nearly two-thirds of the labor force
was located in the field and one-third at the home office, an almost
complete reversal of the proportion that had existed in the early 1970s.
There was little change in those ratios between 1980 and 1983. However,
whereas employment had continued to grow throughout the 1970s, there
was a sharp decline in the first three years of the new decade—nearly
2,000 fewer employees.

The Impact of Decentralization and Technology
on Work and Skills

Phases of Computerization

Ever since its early days, the industry has had to deal with two major
problems: (1) setting up procedures to process the insurance product,
including rating policies, preparing policy documents, processing claims,
and issuing checks and (2) managing the huge archival files associated
with insurance products. Of the various insurance lines offered, property
and casualty, as well as medical products, historically have resulted in
the worst archival problems. Not only is there a need for the unending
reopening of ongoing files (claim processing, annual renewal of policies,
etc.), but insurance companies are required by law to maintain files
long after policies are void (often up to ten years, depending on the
state). Before extensive computerization was achieved, a major difficulty
often was in locating files simply because several departments (billing,
claim processing, underwriting) might have competed for the same file

simultaneously. In addition, there was tremendous redundancy because agents and field offices maintained their own set of files separate from those held at the head office. Typically, insurance companies employed several hundred file clerks and messengers to circulate files among departments. In the usual setup, these positions represented entry-level jobs, fed with a new crop of high school graduates every spring. One company official reported that as late as the early 1970s, the company customarily hired nearly 2,000 high school graduates every summer.

This explains why the industry looked to computer technology since its early commercialization to help solve both processing and paper-shuffling problems. Until the late 1960s and early 1970s, however, applications of mainframe computer technology remained limited in scope. For the most part, early computerized systems were used to automate heavy number-crunching tasks, such as updating actuarial tables, testing new insurance products, handling general ledger work, billing clients, or processing checks. Still, by the late 1960s, some companies had begun experimenting with computerized technology for policy rating and claim processing. Typically the process was cumbersome, however, necessitating mailing keypunch cards or computer tapes from office to office and maintaining both paper files and partially computerized records. In addition, the computerized processing had to be handled by specialized personnel trained in using a relatively complicated technology.

Advances in computerized technology in the early and mid–1970s, involving the introduction of on-line systems, and the development of new memory devices with greatly expanded capacity, made possible a true revolution in the work process of the insurance industry. The first distributed data processing systems were introduced in the early 1970s. By the late 1970s most companies, including the company under study, had on-line systems in the critical areas of underwriting, claim processing, premium calculation, billing, marketing, and mailing.

Most companies set up independent systems in each of these major areas, implying some degree of redundancy from system to system and also some limitation due to the lack of interaccessibility. Still, the computerization of the 1970s did away with the file management problem since records were routinely computerized. The company estimates that by 1984, its medical claim system, one of its largest systems, had in storage somewhere between 17 and 20 million individual files, generating nearly 70,000 daily transactions.

The Impact on the Work Process

Strictly speaking, the impact of computerized technology on productivity has been enormous. As I show later, the absolute number of clerical personnel needed to process transactions at the company began declining steadily after 1980, even though the number of transactions continued to increase. Indeed, newer products have tended to be far more transaction oriented than older ones in part because automated processing makes such products far more feasible than they would have been under manual processing.

Broadly speaking, the reorganization of the production process has been so extensive that some even have argued the industry has now entered a stage in the division of labor that lies "beyond Taylorism" (Appelbaum, 1984). In turn, changes in the division of labor have led to changes in the sequence of job hopping within the firm and have disrupted traditional internal labor markets.

Historically, the work process in the insurance industry had been organized along an assembly-line principle. Since the bulk of the labor force was concentrated in the home office, this made it easier to have the various clerks and professionals involved in a given production process centralized in a single office (Appelbaum, 1984; Baran, 1985).

Baran (1985) describes a typical underwriting process:

> The client policy information gathered by an agent was forwarded to an underwriting department, located either in the home or branch office; the underwriters established a file on the client, evaluated the risk and after determining the risk parameters sent the policy to the rating section where a rater (a skilled clerical employee) calculated the premium charges based on guidelines contained in numerous manuals; sometimes that information had to be communicated back to the agent so that the client could make a decision whether or not to use this particular company; in other cases, the policy went back to the underwriter who reviewed it and then sent it to a typing pool where policy typists prepared the various forms and documents; finally, the policy was mailed back to the agent who forwarded it to the customer. Renewals and policy changes of any kind involved requesting the client file from the file room and sending the policy back through these various stations, although the time involved was usually considerably less.

Similar work processes prevailed in claims and billing. If anything, the tendency during the 1950s and 1960s was to further parcel and fragment work (Baran, 1985). The introduction of early computerized systems did not alter dramatically such a division of labor; it simply added one more fragmented task to the sequence—the keypunching of the data needed for computer processing. This very division of labor formed the base on which the system of internal job ladders rested. The majority of workers were hired in the lowest positions—typically as file clerks and messengers—and moved on over the years to become typing clerks, raters, underwriting assistants, or even underwriters.

Typically, when carriers introduced large-scale distributed systems in the 1970s, they first tried to replicate the old manual procedures with the new systems. In recent years, however, insurers have discovered, the new technology permits them not only to automate many traditional tasks but also to aggregate many tasks into new combinations—in short, to move beyond the old assembly-line concept.

The general tendency in both the industry and the company has been for automation to impact the most heavily the traditional functions both at the very bottom and at the highest levels of the production process. Work reorganization has tended to occur around middle-level clerical processing positions. By eliminating much of the need for manual files, the new generation of technology has done away with much of the need for file clerks and messengers. At the same time, the development of computerized algorithmic procedures has made possible the automation of rating and claim-calculation procedures, leading to the elimination of the traditional positions of raters, claims adjusters, and even assistant underwriters.

At the level of processing, much of the remaining work has been regrouped into a single complete procedure carried out by relatively skilled clerks located in regional processing centers. These centers employ only a few hundred employees, mostly in claims or underwriting, who are supervised by just a few supervisors and managers. Early in the development of the regional processing centers, the company tried using two-person workstations, with a low-level clerk doing much of the data-entry work and a higher-level clerk overseeing the underwriting or the claim-processing procedure. The company also tried using presorting, with routine, simple work sent to one pool of less trained clerks and complex work sent to another pool of better-trained clerks. The company, however, abandoned both ideas because the separation between processing and data entry made it difficult to control mistakes and resulted in high error rates. The separation of easy cases from complex cases also resulted in increased errors due to boredom among workers handling easy cases and high levels of tension among workers continuously handling complex cases.

In recent years, the company has moved away from these earlier experiments, merged the complete work process within one job, eliminated presorting, and moved toward distributing work among groups of clerks on the basis of accounts. Under this system, a small group of clerks handles claim processing for just a few companies. This makes it easy to keep groups of workers up to date about ongoing changes in coverage not programmed into the system. The company also is

TABLE 5.4
Employee Distribution Among Insurance Company Grades, 1983

Grades	Job Description	Number of Employees
1–3	Service workers and low-level clerical (janitors, messengers, file clerks)	1,565
4–8	Benefit approvers (claim policy clerks)	7,485
9–14	Junior professionals and technicians (accounting trainees, actuary trainees, underwriting trainees, etc.)	3,508
15–20	Professionals, managers, and officers	2,108
Total		14,821

Source: Insurance Company data.

moving toward merging customer assistance tasks with processing tasks. Customer assistance is an area which has been extensively transformed. Customer representatives can now "pull out" the record directly on a screen as they talk with customers over the phone, solve problems immediately or key in the codes needed for a claim adjuster to finalize procedures. At present, the company uses separate pools of clerks, but in some of its centers, it is using job rotation to move clerks back and forth from claim-processing to customer representative work. Ultimately, the two positions are likely to be merged.

At the professional level, automation has eliminated many traditional professional or semiprofessional functions. Nowadays, underwriters are needed only in specific, specialized areas. At the same time, however, the product revolution that has occurred in the industry has created openings in actuarial areas for new product development. The introduction of computerized systems has brought with it a demand for computer operators, programmers, and systems analysts. And the multiplication and increasing complexity of products and markets have brought a greater need for professionals in areas such as marketing and sales. These new professionals, however, are increasingly hired directly into junior managerial positions from colleges or professional schools.

The result, in the words of one of the company executives interviewed, has been a marked shift to a two-tier employment structure: a large layer of upper-level clerical workers with limited opportunities for mobility within the company and a large layer of exempt employees with a relatively well developed structure of opportunities. Table 5.4, which breaks down employment by grade, shows this structure. The bottom half of the company's employment structure includes principally benefit approvers (over 7,585 employees in grades 4 to 8) and a few low-level clerical or service-worker positions (1,565 in grades 1 to 3), while the upper half is distributed somewhat evenly between junior professionals (3,503 between grades 9 and 14) and senior professionals and managers (2,263 between grades 15 and the officer level).

The Impact of Change on Employment in the Case Company

The impact of the aforementioned changes on employment opportunities at the company has been profound. I now review first their impact on hiring requirements and opportunities for internal promotion, second employment turnover in the company, and third the sex and race composition of the company's labor force.

Hiring Requirements and Mobility Opportunities

From a firm previously characterized by two main ports of entry, the company has evolved since the 1970s to one characterized by four main ports of entry. Conversely, this increase in the number of entry ports translated into a weakening of traditional internal ladders.

Until the early 1970s, the bulk of the hiring took place at the very bottom entry level (grades 1 and 2), with the company recruiting mostly freshly minted high school graduates. As was mentioned earlier, during its peak years, the company hired nearly 2,000 high school graduates each summer, a number which included "excess hiring" because dropout rates tended to be very high during the first two years (25 percent or more). From that point on most positions, including lower-level professional, supervisory, and middle-managerial promotions, were filled through in-house promotion, although by the late 1960s the company had begun recruiting more actively among college graduates for exempt ranks.

This two-entry system was transformed profoundly during the 1970s. Heavy computerization eliminated much of the need for lower-level clerical work, and today there are far fewer messengers and file clerks. Some hiring is still done at the grade 1 level, but this represents a minor entry post. The main entry post is now at the grade 4 level, directly into benefit approvers positions. To staff these positions, the company looks for skilled clerical personnel which it finds either among older, experienced workers; younger workers with an associate degree from a community college; or even graduates from a four-year college. Grade changes between 4 and 9 are typically associated with seniority and individual productivity. They translate into higher earnings but do not on average indicate any major differences in skill level.

The next major entry point is at grade 9 or 10 in which the company hires accounting trainees, actuarial trainees, and other junior professionals typically with a four-year degree in economics, business, or specialized fields such as computer science (for its systems area) or mathematics and statistics (in actuary). Many can hope to move into positions of higher responsibility, although since the mid–1970s, the company has tended to seek increasingly outside its ranks individuals with high-level specialized skills. Today, it recruits actively at professional schools to find individuals with specialization in law (growing demand linked partly to industry deregulation and partly to increasing litigation), computer systems, investment and finance (increased demand for MBAs and financial analysts in the investment division of the firm), etc.

The increasing emphasis on formal credentials at various grade levels, the disappearance of traditional bridge skills such as those of rating and routine underwriting, as well as the geographical separation of the regional processing centers from the home office, have all acted to bring about a two-tier structure, as suggested by executives in the company itself. Regionalization has reinforced the process because the tendency has been to move clerical processing jobs to the regional center and maintain many of the junior professional jobs at the head office. Under the current setup, opportunities for mobility in the regional processing centers are limited to a few supervisory positions. Typically, regional processing centers employ 400 to 450 people and are run by a regional benefit officer with four division managers under him or her and four section managers under each division manager, each supervising approximately 25 to 30 people. In addition, a small technical support staff runs the computers, and a small personnel support staff hires, appraises, and trains personnel. Thus far, section and division managers have tended to come from the ranks, although in recent years the tendency has been to hire division managers from the outside labor market. The capacity for the company to run regional centers with a low ratio of supervisors to production personnel has in part been helped by the use of quality-circle management methods.

In selecting locations for its regional processing centers, the company has followed a pattern very much in evidence in the rest of the industry, and has tended to look for local markets where labor and other operating costs (rents, utilities) are lower than in the home office location and where a steady supply of clerical labor can be expected. The tendency has been to move into medium-sized metropolitan centers and to look for older women or younger women graduating from community colleges. In two instances, Fresno and Colorado Springs, the company has turned

to relatively small urban centers. Both communities have military in-
stallations and provide an ample supply of wives of enlisted men and
retired military clerks who are willing to work a few additional years.
The advantage of hiring among these two groups is that these workers
are unlikely to demand much mobility, something the company can no
longer offer. The women's ability to stay in steady jobs is partly limited
by the frequent relocation of their husbands, and the older men are
likely to view these jobs as short term.

In addition to altering the nature of the linkage between home office
and field jobs, regionalization and technological change also have acted
to change job opportunities in district offices where the sales effort is
concentrated. Traditionally, life insurance carriers have sold life insurance
products through independent agents. However, a number of the large
carriers, including the case company, have long relied in part on their
own sales force.

In the company, agents are organized by sales districts, with several
districts per agency. Agencies in turn are grouped by region within a
six-region system that matches the regional division for the processing
side of the business.

Agents are recruited among people with a college education and
preferably among people who have special linkages with specific social
networks that can give them a base of prospective clients to start from.
For the first four years, agents are paid partly on salary, partly on
commission, with the share of salary decreasing over the years. Beginning
in the fifth year, they are shifted completely to commissions. Turnover
is very high in the first couple of years because it is difficult to get
started in the business. Agents report to district managers who are
experienced agents and who continue to handle their own clients but
also do some administrative work—mostly hiring new agents and
training—for which they receive a partial salary. District managers report
to agency managers, typically one such manager per agency, although
the largest agencies have two managers (i.e., a total of 190 managers
for the 120 agencies). In turn, agency managers answer to a regional
vice-president.

At the agency level, clerical staff was trimmed to the bare minimum
once the general-service offices were closed and merged into the regional
processing centers. Clerical work associated with agencies is now limited
to agents' inquiries to the regional centers for policy quotes, requests
for billing, policy underwriting, and agency bookkeeping. The work is
computerized on minicomputers that are matched overnight in batch
mode with the regional center computers. In addition, the company is
helping agents purchase PCs, which they typically use to maintain their
customer files. The company is also experimenting with introducing a

system in the agencies to computerize the policy-application process directly at the stage of the agent.

Turnover and Employment Stability

Although the company did not release data on employment turnover, it would be interesting to see if the company experienced a rise in turnover among clerical personnel with the decline in opportunities for mobility resulting from regionalization and new technology. As a piece of indirect evidence, in her book, *No Room at the Top*, Burris (1983) studied in detail a large sample of benefit approver clerks in a large insurance firm and found a marked tendency towards increasing levels of turnover.

Short of appropriate quantitative evidence, information gathered during interviews nevertheless suggest that in the late 1970s the company experienced difficulty in adjusting to rapid productivity gains. Technology helped transform the work process and bring about major productivity increases in an environment in which the output of the industry was growing slowly. In addition, the regionalization program forced major geographical adjustments.

In the home office, while the company sought to handle the impact of the regionalization effort through attrition and relocation assistance, it became clear in the late 1970s that the program would not move as fast as the company had expected unless drastic measures were taken. The company pushed through a program of job elimination and layoffs handled partly through early retirement and partly through job-search assistance. The purpose of the program was to cut down the number of middle-level personnel (mostly raters and low-level administrators) who were most directly affected by technological change. This same group, however, was also mostly static since many were mature workers who had advanced through the ranks. Several hundred workers were forced out during the period.

At the field level, the closing of general-service offices and their merger into central offices has been slow. Nearly ten years after its inception, the program is not yet complete, reflecting partly the resistance that the company has met in implementing the program.

Barrier to Entry: Sex and Race

Table 5.5 and Table 5.6 show employment transformation at the Company over the eleven-year period of 1971 to 1982. As indicated in Table 5.5, there was a marked shift from relatively lower- to relatively higher-skilled occupations during those years. Total employment grew by 26 percent, but employment among professional and technical per-

TABLE 5.5
Occupational Distribution of Employment: The Insurance Company, 1971 and 1982

	1971	1982	% Change
Officials and Managers	2,848	3,163	11.1
Professional and Technicians	2,665	6,124	130.0
Sales	1,817	3,234	78.0
Office and Clerical	8,435	8,157	−3.3
Crafts, Operatives, Laborers,			
and Service Workers	851	259	−69.6
Total	16,616	20,937	26.0

Sources: Insurance Company, *EEO-1 Reports,* 1971 and 1982.

sonnel and sales personnel grew by 130 percent and 78 percent, respectively. Employment among office clerical and blue-collar and service-worker occupations, however, declined by 3.3 percent and 69.6 percent, respectively.

The company also made great strides in its employment of women and minorities. The share of white men in the company's labor force decreased by nearly 10 percent (from 42.0 down to 32.2 percent), with the greatest relative gains made by minority women and minority men (although the latter are still trailing minority women in terms of overall share). In general, there were significant advances by white women, minority men, and minority women in the professional and technical personnel group—the fastest-growing group. In addition, minority men improved their representation as managers, and the number of white and minority women in sales increased, although still had a long way to go to improve its representation among agents. This was confirmed through interviews with a woman executive in the company who observed that traditionally the agent system had been male dominated and that the highest-ranking women had tended to come from technical areas such as systems and actuary. In 1983 only 2 out of 190 women were agency managers. The proportions were barely better among district managers and only slightly better among agents.

The data shown in the two tables do not fully capture important recent changes; in particular, they don't show the impact on women of the clerical downturn which began in 1980 as a result of the regionalization program and the productivity increases brought about by the new technology. Table 5.7 shows detailed employment data on white and

TABLE 5.6
Occupational Distribution of Major Groups of Workers: The Insurance Company, 1982 and 1971

	1982						1971					
	Total[a]		White Men	White Women	Minority Men	Minority Women	Total[a]		White Men	White Women	Minority Men	Minority Women
	#	%					#	%				
Managers	3,163	15.1	76.8[b]	12.0	9.1	2.1	2,848	17.1	86.8	9.7	3.3	0.3
Professional and Technical	6,124	29.2	28.4	47.5	7.7	16.4	2,665	16.0	61.2	33.2	2.6	2.7
Sales	3,234	15.4	60.7	16.5	17.2	5.6	1,817	10.9	81.6	1.7	16.3	0.5
Clerical	8,157	39.0	5.1	65.8	3.2	25.9	8,435	50.8	11.8	66.0	3.5	18.7
Other Occupations	259	1.2	75.0	2.3	19.3	3.5	851	5.1	44.8	24.7	21.9	8.5
Total	20,937	100.0	32.2	43.9	7.8	16.1	16,616	100.0	42.0	41.9	5.6	10.5

[a] By comparison to the figures shown in Table 5.3, sales agents employed by the company are included here and are counted mostly in the Sales occupational group.
[b] Each line adds to 100 percent.

TABLE 5.6
(Continued)
Occupational Underrepresentation or Overrepresentation of Major Groups of Workers: 1982 and 1971

	1982				1971			
	White Men	White Women	Minority Men	Minority Women	White Men	White Women	Minority Men	Minority Women
Managers	2.39	0.27	1.16	0.13	2.07	0.23	0.59	0.03
Professional and Technical	0.88	1.08	0.99	1.02	1.46	0.79	0.46	0.26
Sales	1.88	0.38	2.21	0.35	1.94	0.04	2.91	0.05
Clerical	0.16	1.50	0.41	1.61	0.28	1.58	0.63	1.78
Other Occupations	2.33	0.05	2.47	0.22	1.06	0.59	3.91	0.81

Note: Occupational representation is measured as the ratio of the share of employment of a given group in a given occupation divided by its share of total employment. A ratio above 1 indicates overrepresentation; below 1, underrepresentation.

Sources: Insurance Company, EEO-1 Reports, 1971 and 1982.

TABLE 5.7
Employment of White Women and Minority Women: The Insurance Company,
1979–1982

	White Women			Minority Women		
	All Employment	Clerical	Professional and Technical	All Employment	Clerical	Professional and Technical
1979	8,342	5,126	2,425	3,140	2,182	675
1980	8,969	5,590	2,585	3,475	2,366	804
1981	9,019	5,534	2,753	3,446	2,321	913
1982	9,191	5,365	2,909	3,376	2,115	1,004

Sources: Insurance Company, *EEO-1 Reports,* 1979, 1980, 1981, and 1982.

minority women in clerical and professional and technical occupations
for the years 1977 through 1982. Over 90 percent of the women were
employed in these two major groups. What the data show is that the
downturn in clerical employment had a more severe impact on minority
women than on white women. White women made up the losses in
clerical through gains in professional and technical positions so that
their employment continued to grow in absolute terms (+222 net jobs
between 1980 and 1982). Minority women, however, could not com-
pensate clerical losses to the same extent, and their overall number
declined (−99 net jobs between 1980 and 1982). This simply reflects
the fact that the loss of clerical jobs due to productivity gains and the
regionalization program impacted particularly seriously this group of
women for whom such positions represented a relatively larger share
of the employment.

Ongoing Changes

In looking to the future, one gets a strong sense that the company,
like many others in its industry, will continue to experience pains and
stresses as it searches for a reasonable course through uncharted terrain.

On the market side, product competition in financial industries is
unlikely to abate, and no one can predict where the chips will fall.
There is a strong realization by the company that the old days are over
and that new market niches must be identified to sustain future growth.
In this respect, the company has made major efforts in recent years to
strengthen its resources as a pension fund manager and to expand its
involvement in real estate development and financing.

On the human resource side, while the years ahead may not produce quite the same level of turmoil as that which resulted from the decentralization program, the going is unlikely to be smooth either. Continued improvements in automated back-office processing systems are most likely to pressure the company to reduce further its clerical employment. Within the past year or so, Prudential, the largest firm in the industry and the traditional trendsetter, announced a dramatic program of concentration in its regional processing centers that will involve merging its six centers into three. Several of the executives interviewed for this study indicated that the company might soon have to consider similar measures. In addition, a major concern today is for the relative decline of traditional individual life insurance products in favor of sophisticated ones, for example, those that are linked to money management. As a result of this decline, the company may have to ask some hard questions at the professional and managerial levels regarding its customary sales agent system whose future as a distribution medium in the age of automated teller machines (ATMs) and electronic networking might very much be in doubt (Noyelle, forthcoming).

6

Market and Job Segmentation in the New Economy

In reappraising the usefulness and validity of dual labor market theory, it is important to remember that it remains, first and foremost, historically grounded. Contrary to neoclassical theories of the labor market that portends to develop timeless and spaceless conceptualizations, dual labor market theory was formulated originally to describe U.S. labor markets at a particular moment in their historical development.

In 1982 Gordon, Edwards, and Reich published an important book, *Segmented Work, Divided Workers* (1982), in which they attempted to situate dual labor market theory within a broad historical perspective of the transformation of U.S. labor markets. The authors argued that the period of industrial dual labor markets, which they referred to as the period of *segmentation*, represented the third major stage in the transformation of U.S. labor markets under capitalism. Specifically, the authors suggested that three overlapping stages had shaped the development of labor markets since the early nineteenth century: *initial proletarianization* from the 1820s to the 1890s, *homogenization* from the 1870s to the onset of World War II, and *segmentation* from the 1920s to the present. For each of these three stages, Gordon et al. identified a "period of exploration," a "period of consolidation," and a "period of decay," with considerable overlapping between a new period of exploration and the period of decay of the previous stage. This explains the juxtaposition in the authors' dating of the three stages.

In broad terms, Gordon et al. described the period of *initial proletarianization* as that period during which wage labor became the dominant manner of organizing production, necessitating the formation of a large supply of wage workers from a previously nonproletarian population. The following period, *homogenization*, occurred when factory owners fought to wrestle away from craft workers the management of the production process in order to control pace and productivity. This was

97

achieved in part through more extensive mechanization of production making possible the substitution of craftsmen with semiskilled workers. Finally, the period of *segmentation* found its origin in the unionization drive of the 1920s and 1930s and in employers' responses to some of the demands of unionism. In the view of Gordon et al., this led to a segmentation of the labor market between mostly unionized core employers and mostly nonunionized peripheral firms and prevented the growth of a unified and, thus, more threatening working class.

Gordon et al. brought their study to a close with an observation that remained mostly a hypothesis; that "the structure of segmentation has begun to decay and . . . explorations are underway that will significantly alter existing institutions in each of the three principal labor segments" (Gordon et al., 1982, p. 226). I believe that the three case studies presented in this book go a long way in substantiating their hypothesis, even though they might fall short of providing all the elements needed to characterize the next stage in the development of U.S. labor markets.

In the following pages, I attempt to piece together a preliminary sketch of the emerging era. Perhaps this period should be called the *era of professionalization and paraprofessionalization*, to account for the key dimensions of change, namely that mobility is becoming increasingly occupation driven rather than firm driven, and that, as a result, the systems of social rewards and cultural references are increasingly defined by professional peer groups rather than employers.

The use of the terms professionalization and paraprofessionalization is not meant to mystify the transformation under way, nor is it meant to imply that everyone has or will achieve the social status of a Wall Street lawyer or a brain surgeon. Nevertheless, in one form or another the trend toward professionalization is extending far beyond the few established professions. It has not only pervaded employment in the primary independent job segment, but it is similarly expanding into the primary subordinate segment. And even though the trend is clearly leaving large areas of low-skilled employment untouched, it is possible to argue that in the long run the relative importance of such employment will continue to decrease as automation proceeds, giving an even greater weight to the new professional and paraprofessional worker. Note that predicting a shrinkage of low-skilled employment is different from predicting a shrinkage of low-paid employment. I return to this point later.

While it may be tempting to draw some parallels between today's professional and paraprofessional workers and the craft workers of earlier days, it may be important to realize that thus far each seems to have had a history of transformation which stands in contrast to the other. The history of the craft worker was largely one of subjugation to the owners of capital, first by bringing craftsmen into the wage labor system (the stage of proletarianization) and second by removing from craftsmen a great deal of the control over the production process (the stage of homogenization). By comparison, the history of professionalization may well be one of emerging relative independence vis-à-vis the owners of capital reflecting at once: (1) the growing importance of knowledge-based inputs in processes of production; (2) the difficulty of traditional capitalism to assert its control over new critical inputs; (3) the desire of firms to increase their flexibility within markets by purchasing "increments of expertise" as needed rather than by hiring people to which they must become committed; and (4) the concomitant attempt by occupational groups to reestablish control over blocks of knowledge as a way to enchance their leverage in the marketplace. The rise in self-employment not only among professionals but also among paraprofessionals such as nurses, book editors, service repair specialists, PBX installers, and many others is in my opinion one trend among others that is indicative of these changes.

In the remainder of this chapter, I attempt to organize what is known and what has been learned from the case studies about market and job segmentation in the new economic era. In the following three sections, I cover, respectively, the new market fragmentation, some changing characteristics of jobs, and the changing dynamics of labor markets. I conclude with some observations about the changing nature of job segments.

A New Market Fragmentation

Bluestone and his colleagues (1981) were among the first to point out the emerging contradictions within dual labor market theory, especially in regard to the basic linkages between the core economy and primary job segments on the one hand and the peripheral economy and secondary job segments on the other. Taking cues from their studies of the retail industry, Bluestone and Stevenson (in Wilkinson, 1981) argued that conventional dual labor market theory was unable to explain the formation of what they called *hybrid firms:*

> Job structures in the department store industry represent a hybrid: a very high (and steadily increasing) proportion of the selling jobs fall within the secondary market; the expanding number of administrative and managerial job slots are in the primary. The question to be raised—one that has not yet received sufficient attention within labor market segmentation theory—is: Why is it that, while some "core" firms find it desirable to structure all their jobs to fall within the primary market, other "core"

firms find it desirable to locate more of their jobs within the secondary
market while maintaining a primary market for the rest? (p. 4)

Not only does the case study of R. H. Macy & Co. confirm Bluestone
and Stevenson's finding about the department store industry, but the
cases of New York Telephone and the insurance company suggest that
new models of firms are emerging in other industries as well. The three
cases indicate that these quintessential core firms are attempting to
minimize their traditional commitment to primary workers, be it in
terms of guaranteed wage and salary growth; opportunities for occupational mobility; or secure, long-term employment (I return to this
issue shortly). The three case studies also show that new firms are
emerging out of the transformation of the old core firms once characterized
both by their exclusive employment of primary workers and a strong
long-term commitment vis-à-vis such employees.

In all three cases there is a clear relationship between this transformation and the intensification of competition. In the department store
industry, as I have indicated, while the postwar period saw the emergence
of many large chains, the result was often *more* rather than *less* competition, with different organizations (department stores, national merchandisers, discounters, specialty chains) using different modes of production to compete, often in the same markets. In the telephone industry,
a principal purpose of deregulation, and ultimately of the dismantling
of AT&T, was to restore competition. In insurance, price and product
deregulation brought much the same outcome.

Under industrial dualism, the capacity of core firms to offer primary
employment was in large measure related to their ability to operate in
an oligopolistic or monopolistic environment (e.g., the steel, automobile,
local gas and electric utilities, and telephone industries). Business fluc-
tuations could be absorbed through different shock absorbers: by shifting
the burden of employment adjustment to suppliers in the peripheral
economy; by raising prices to make up for the slack in demand; or,
when needed, by temporarily laying off some workers under a system
of unemployment insurance largely paid out of the long-run profits of
the firm.

Under deregulation and internationalization, the return to price competition in many sectors of the economy has undermined considerably
the capacity of core firms to continue to operate in a sheltered oligopolistic
environment. As a result, a new economic fragmentation is now emerging
between sunrise and sunset industries, substituting for that between
core and periphery industries. *Sunrise industries* tend to develop in
highly competitive environments. They include, but are not limited to,
many new industries and many industries that once were considered

part of the periphery. Many service industries fall into this category. By contrast, *sunset industries* tend to include those that remain shackled by their past and have difficulties repositioning themselves vis-à-vis the new markets and the new economy. Many of these industries were once part of the core. It is almost as if there has been a complete reversal in the relationship between core and periphery, with the periphery comprising the services and high-tech industries now taking the lead. It is not quite the same, however, if only because the size-of-firm dimension, which played an important role in distinguishing between the old core and periphery, now seems less relevant. In addition, some old core companies are clearly showing signs of success in their transformation to sunrise firms.

Expanding on concepts similar to those suggested by Piore and Sabel (1984), Christopherson and Storper (1985) suggest that an important feature of the transformation from sunset to sunrise status involves what they call *vertical disintegration*. Under old-fashioned vertical integration, large firms sought to establish control over both a large scope of activities in the production process and a large scale of the production of specific outputs. Under vertical disintegration, firms tend to specialize in types or classes of production rather than in the production of large quantities of specific outputs as in mass production. The essence of the firm becomes flexible production. One result, according to Christopherson and Storper, is that while vertical integration emphasized the internalization of many transactions within the firm, vertical disintegration emphasizes greater reliance on market mechanisms. In their own terms, the new economic structure emphasizes the continuing "mix and match of specialized production firms to produce continuously changing outputs." While the authors take their cues from their study of the transformation of the U.S. motion picture industry, the companies studied for this book each point to transforming tendencies similar to those suggested by Christopherson and Storper. In the telephone industry, the tendency is toward vertical disintegration; in retailing and financial services industries, the tendency is toward making production more flexible, more focused on market segments, and less dependent on specific outputs.

Consistent with the tendency toward vertical disintegration, in sunrise industries organizational layers are few, and firms depend overwhelmingly on the external labor markets to locate high-, middle-, or low-skilled labor as needed; in sunset industries, firms continue to depend on multilayered organizations with built-in internal job laddering. In sunrise firms, the emphasis is on assembling modules of expertise (professional or paraprofessional) and simple labor in various combinations rather than on organizing layers of authority as in sunset firms.

In addition, in sunrise industries, employment systems are less and less a function of the old dichotomy between large and small firms. Decreasingly employment systems are a function of the firm's type of production rather than size. In the accounting industry, for example, both small and large firms rely principally on highly skilled professionals, while in retailing, almost regardless of size, there now is extensive use of the hybrid model suggested by Bluestone and his associates.

In sunset industries, the fate of a particular firm may hinge largely on its capacity to respond to new competition by adopting features of the emerging new employment systems. The automobile industry is by far the most conspicuous example of a sunset industry that is attempting rejuvenation not only with new products and new production technologies but also with the transformation of its industrial and labor relations systems. The far-reaching organizational restructuring announced by General Motors for its new Saturn division is a case in point (*Business Week*, 1985). This development, however, simply follows employment changes that have been in progress in the industry since the late 1970s (Katz, 1985; Bertrand and Noyelle, 1985). In contrast, the inability of the mainstream steel industry to move away decisively from an old, core employment structure might ultimately undermine its role. The result of this inability is that tomorrow's markets are likely to be dominated either by new firms that have emerged and grown outside the traditional industry (the mini mills) or by foreign firms that have succeeded in penetrating the domestic markets. Still, to a large extent, the transformation of industries from sunset to sunrise will not be limited to manufacturing but will involve many other firms and industries, as suggested directly by the three case studies presented in this book.

Last, the use of the new competitive environment does not imply that large firms are suddenly disappearing. It simply means that deregulation and increasing internationalization are likely to guarantee in the years ahead that a sufficient number of large firms remain in most markets to ensure high levels of competition.

Some Changing Characteristics of Jobs

Renewed, across-the-board competition is undoubtedly one factor that is putting pressure on how jobs are organized, mostly toward a loosening of traditional tenure-like bonds between firms and employees. As the case studies demonstrate, also driving the reorganization of jobs is the introduction of new technology—by changing the nature of skills and the demand for labor—and the expansion of higher education—by transforming the structure of the labor supply to such an extent that firms must alter their hiring practices.

Increasing Turnover

In general, there is broad evidence of a rise in employee turnover, pointing to the loosening of worker attachment to specific firms. In the chapter on R. H. Macy & Co., I reported on data assembled by Bluestone et al. (1981) suggesting a steady rise of turnover in the department store industry from the 1950s to 1970s. The lack of company data made it difficult to analyze the turnover record for each of the three firms. In general, however, the trends revealed by Bluestone et al. have tended to be confirmed by others and for other sectors. A few years back, Ann Crittendon noted in the *New York Times* (1980) that according to a National Bureau of Economic Research study, by the late 1970s American workers were holding an average of ten or more jobs between the ages of 16 and 65 and with the exception of an increasingly smaller group of workers that stayed with their jobs for long periods of time, job hopping was increasing. This was confirmed by a *Personnel Journal* survey that was quoted in the same article showing that between 1963 and 1980, the average tenure on a job had declined from 4.6 to 3.6 years. Likewise, Rogers (1985), a student of high technology industries, quotes turnover rates of approximately 30 percent per year among professional and technical personnel in the electronics industry in the Silicon Valley. Rogers points to the fact that the very dynamism of the industry rests in large part on a high degree of openness, which makes it possible for continuous startups of new projects and new businesses.

Technology and Skills

No issue in recent years has brought about a more heated debate among economists than that concerning the impact of technology on skills.

The controversy began nearly ten years ago when Harry Braverman, a self-taught economist who for many years was on the editorial board of *Monthly Review*, published his *Labor and Monopoly Capital: The Degradation of Work in the Twentieth Century* (1974).

Throughout the twentieth century, the relentless drive for productivity gains by capitalists had led, according to Braverman, to an ever-finer Taylorization of work, a continuous decline in skill requirements, and the endless degradation of work. Technology was used in a largely monolithic fashion, as a major ingredient in the general process of Taylorization and deskilling, that is, in the process of work degradation. To Braverman's credit, his book contained some brilliant insights, not the least of which were his attempts to reach beyond the labor economist's conventional focus on blue-collar workers and develop a deeper un-

TABLE 6.1
Occupational Distribution of Employed Workers, 1960–1982 (in percentages)

	1960	1970	1975	1982
White-Collar and Service Workers	55.5	60.7	63.5	67.5
Managers and Administrators	10.7	10.5	10.5	11.5
Professional and Technicians	11.4	14.2	15.1	17.0
Sales Workers	6.4	6.2	6.4	6.6
Clerical Workers	14.8	17.4	17.8	18.5
Service Workers	12.2	12.4	13.7	13.8
Blue-Collar Workers	36.6	35.3	33.0	29.7
Craft and Kindred	13.0	12.9	12.9	12.3
Operatives	18.2	17.7	15.2	12.9
Nonfarm Laborers	5.4	4.7	4.9	4.5
Farm Workers	7.9	4.0	3.4	2.7
Services as Percent of U.S. Nonagricultural Employment	62.3	63.1	70.9	73.3

Source: U.S. Department of Labor, Bureau of Labor Statistics, *Employment and Earnings* (Washington, D.C.: Government Printing Office, various issues).

derstanding of the economy's shift to white-collar work and service-industry employment.

It may be argued, however, that Braverman's analysis was influenced by an earlier, qualitatively different phase of computerization (the commercialization of the first generations of mainframe computers) during which computers did have some downskilling impact, especially on groups of low-level clerical workers such as keypunchers and the like. Nevertheless, it also can be said that Braverman's gloomy assessment did not square fully either with the steady rise of education in our society or with the general upgrading of the overall occupational structure, as witnessed by the continuing buildup of employment in occupational groupings such as administrators, professionals, and technicians (see Table 6.1). Clearly, the occupational shifts revealed by the data implied more than simply inflation in educational credentials or inflation in job titles.

In the broad sense then, I would argue that Braverman was wrong in that he was attempting to project the dynamics of transformation associated with the stage of *homogenization* (Gordon et al., 1982) beyond a time when this very dynamic had faded already. In the end, Braverman failed to see the potential of technology, especially the latest wave of computerization, for shifting (1) the nature of the labor process largely away from Taylorization and (2) the nature of the skill demanded to operate such technology away from processing skills toward problem-solving skills (see Chapter 2).

Indeed, Braverman notwithstanding, the bulk of the evidence accumulated in recent years by other researchers (Adler, 1984; Adler & Bowers, 1983; Hirschhorn, 1984; Appelbaum, 1984; Baran, 1985; Bertrand and Noyelle, 1985; Noyelle, forthcoming) suggests broad upskilling, even though downskilling might continue to occur in some situations. As Adler (1985) argues, the ultimate objective of the firm is to maximize profits, not to degrade work. So if profits can be maximized through upskilling rather than downskilling, why not?

This having been said, it is important to recognize the tendency of firms to first use the new technology within the framework of the old division of labor. In Chapter 5, I noted that it took several years for the insurance company to begin moving away from an old division of work based on step-by-step parcelization toward a new one based on some notion of multifunctional work.

Likewise, there have been numerous criticisms of the telephone company's highly Tayloristic approach to work organization in its ASCCs, emphasizing not only parcelization but also electronic monitoring of worker productivity (Howard, 1980). Nevertheless, one must question how long this approach can be sustained. Hirschhorn (forthcoming) finds that such work organization tends to be highly counterproductive and that there are enormous pressures to move away from it. While the technical knowledge demanded from switchmen is high, their level of mental stress is considerable. Workers never follow through the resolution of a given problem; they deal only with parts of it. The result is stress, frustration, and a lacking sense of achievement. Finally, as I noted in Chapter 4, it is also true that in the areas of operator and directory assistance, the telephone company has used automated equipment in a deskilling mode. In the long run, however, most of these jobs are destined to disappear through automation. Admittedly, this will necessitate the replacement of the remaining semiautomatic exchanges with fully automated ones (at this point, mostly international exchanges) and the displacement of directory assistance personnel with widespread videotext systems, such as those being introduced in France, Japan, and Great Britain.

In the insurance company, the aim is to automate the data-entry process, including the interface between the agent and the customer that is where data directly first enters the system. I noted at the end of the last chapter that the case company is experimenting with a computerized application process handled directly by the agent. Other carriers are moving in the same direction. In medical insurance, for example, Blue Cross–Blue Shield of Greater New York can now enter much of its data automatically by connecting its computers directly to those of hospitals in its coverage area.

In short, the tendency is to automate low-skilled jobs and retain those jobs with relatively high skills. The latter are likely to fall into one of the following two categories: (1) old jobs that are extensively transformed and upgraded in conjunction with the introduction of the new technology, for example, indoor craft jobs at the telephone company, claim examiners and agents at the insurance firm, and buyers at Macy's or (2) new jobs that emerge out of the new need to manage the interface between customers and highly automated processing systems, as in the case of branch-bank sales personnel (platform personnel) whose main function is to inform consumers about available product options and their use through ATMs (Noyelle, forthcoming).

From the standpoint of this analysis, it is important to point (1) to the linkages between this transformation of skills and the professionalization of the labor force and (2) to the fact that this trend toward professionalization extends far beyond jobs at the top of the occupational structure and reaches deep into middle-level occupational ranks. While I took note of this transformation in this book, my research indicates similar tendencies in financial services industries (Noyelle, forthcoming). Hirschhorn (1984) suggests a similar interpretation of the transformation of work in typing pools:

> The typing pool was a transitional solution to the problem of integrating computers into office work. As long as the price of hardware and software remained high, it paid companies to purchase dedicated work processors and create a group of specialized typists who did nothing but input text. The high cost of the processors was justified by the economies of specialization. But the declining cost of computer hardware and software is giving rise to the integrated work station in which operators manipulate words, pictures and data together to create, or "publish" documents of high visual quality. Moreover, as managers learn to do their own keyboarding the office "operators" increasingly *supervise* a document production process, rather than operate *within* it. They monitor the office machinery while negotiating with and serving users.

> Indeed, it seems as if three para-professions may be emerging from the increasingly obsolete secretarial role, the para-publisher, the para-librarian and the para-manager. The first supervises the document production process, the second supervises file and index management, with particular references to cross referencing, and the third prepares budgets, monitors master-

calendar preparation and maintains such control system data bases, as productivity and time records.

Productivity and Pay

An additional implication of the transformation of the division of labor is the move toward job designs in which workers deal with entire processes at once rather than with isolated tasks and subtasks, and toward arrangements in which an individual's work is likely to take place within the context of team work, with some degree of inter-changeability among team members.

A recent Organization of Economic Cooperation and Development (OECD) study on technological change in manufacturing industries, including the automobile industry, concludes that there is "increasing emphasis on individual production workers to be able to perform many tasks in the framework of a team." (OECD, 1984). Although this point was not brought out specifically in the case studies, there is evidence that the same trend is found among service industries, including the financial industries where back-office employees using automated systems often work in teams on portfolios of customers (Noyelle, forthcoming).

One implication is that productivity gains are becoming more difficult to link directly to work flow improvements attributable to a specific task and a specific worker. This is not to say that those companies that continue to operate with a mind-set associated with the old, fragmented division of labor will not continue to try to identify, reward, or tax productivity improvement or deterioration on an individual basis. I mentioned the case of electronic monitoring of telephone operators in Chapter 4 and individual productivity wage-setting procedures in some of the back offices of the insurance company studied in Chapter 5. Nevertheless, the broad tendency is to recognize that productivity gains are coming about in quite different ways than in the past to and to identify pay systems that can reward accordingly. In the process, what emerges are various attempts by firms to move away from a simple wage system toward the development of compensation systems that reward employees collectively for group productivity increases. Some firms go as far as eliminating wages, putting everyone on salary, and rewarding everyone for the company's progress through stock ownership; others are not as daring but try to reach out to more employees through vastly expanded stock-option programs (Bertrand & Noyelle, 1985; *New York Times*, 1985). Still other firms complement the pay of waged workers through direct profit-sharing plans such as Improshare or indirect reward systems such as the employee stock ownership plan (ESOP) (Bertrand & Noyelle, 1985). Clearly, however, there is indication that the compensation system is undergoing major changes, although in the short term not necessarily always to the immediate benefit of all (see Chapter 7).

The Changing Dynamics of Mobility:
A Labor Supply Perspective

One useful way to assess the extent of the transformation under way is to identify its impact on the dynamics of job competition. This is done tentatively in the following sections in which I point to changing interactions among back-office employees in the billing and processing offices of firms, such as the insurance firm and the telephone company studied in this book; sales clerks from the retail sector, including those found at R. H. Macy & Co.; and executive and professional personnel from service industries.

While these examples are not meant to encompass the whole range of possible job competition developing in the new economy, they are, nevertheless, symptomatic of some of the new interactions that have developed. In addition, they highlight work situations in which great numbers of women and minority workers have found employment.

The Reorganization of Back-Office Employment

Throughout the 1950s and 1960s, banks, insurance companies, utilities, and other organizations with large processing facilities hired large numbers of youths directly out of high school to staff entry-level clerical positions of messenger and file clerk in their back offices. Thereafter, each new crop of workers was trained in house, and would move up the work ladder as it matured.

In retrospect, this dynamic was altered dramatically during the 1970s, as the reorganization of back-office work led to the elimination of the old entry-level jobs. In Chapter 5, I pointed to the impact of these changes on the hiring of youths in the case study insurance company. In a recent study of the New York City labor market, Bailey and Waldinger (1984) found that of the nearly 40,000 jobs lost by youths in New York City during the decade of 1970–1980, nearly half of the loss were attributable to the elimination of filing clerks, messenger clerks, and similar positions in local utilities (telephone, gas, and electric), banks, and insurance firms; the other half, to the contraction of the city's economy during those years.

In addition to the elimination of low-level entry jobs, two other trends developed as a result of the widespread introduction of distributed data processing during the 1970s and early 1980s.

First, distributed data processing helped in the relocation of back offices away from the central cities of large and very large metropolitan centers where they had been concentrated historically. As I noted in Chapter 5, this development seems to have worked against minority women. Minority women who had made great gains in the clerical ranks of such firms during the 1970s suddenly found themselves left behind in the inner cities where they traditionally have resided. In addition, as employers sought to relocate their back-office facilities in areas where operating costs (rent, utilities) and overall labor costs were lower, they also looked for areas with infrastructures of colleges and community colleges that could help them prepare new crops of employees, retrain an existing pool of skilled workers, or both.

Second, the restructuring and relocation of back-office work contributed to closing off opportunities to move from clerical to professional positions from within the ranks, undermining some of the gains that women and minority workers had achieved in the early and mid–1970s as a result of the EEO focus on opening access to internal labor markets. Women and minority workers who seek to enter upper-level positions must now do it through the college route. Overwhelmingly, it has been white women, mostly from middle-class backgrounds, who have learned to profit from this change. Again, the comparison of the recent employment experience of white women and minority women at the insurance company (Chapter 5) emphasizes this dimension of the change.

The Transformation of Retailing Employment

The case study of R. H. Macy & Co. developed in Chapter 3 underscores the fact that early on in the postwar period much of the employment expansion in the retail industry was built on women—first white women, later minority women. While large retailing organizations were leaders in discovering underutilized pools of women, especially in the suburbs, their discovery did not go unnoticed forever. As we just have seen, large clerical organizations in the late 1970s began seeking actively these same women by relocating back-office facilities in the suburban ring of large cities. In the process, however, they put new pressures on the labor market of adult women, which, in turn, contributed to a shift among retail organizations toward accelerated hiring of high school youths. This shift was fueled further by the many youths who became available as they found other industries increasingly difficult to enter short of educational credentials higher than a high school diploma.

This shift, however, channeled a great many youths into jobs demanding limited skills, offering few opportunities for extensive on-the-job training, and extremely limited opportunities for upward mobility.

As in other industries, the transformation of the job structure in retailing in the late 1960s led to an almost complete break in the link between sales positions and higher-level professional and managerial positions (department managers, buyers, store managers, etc.). As a result, the burden of finding mobility opportunities now rests on youth themselves, and no longer on employers. Here again, we find that those workers, including women and minority workers, that have progressed into higher-level positions have done so through the educational route rather than through internal labor markets.

A Look at the Aggregate Data

To further highlight the dynamics just described, I prepared two sets of aggregate data. Table 6.2, based on 1970 and 1980 census data, presents an industry shift-share analysis for six major groups of workers: youths (aged 16 to 19), black females, Hispanic females, white females, black males, and Hispanic males. For each group, employment growth (or decline) in an industry is disaggregated among its three components: (1) growth (or decline) associated with the relative growth (or decline) of the industry in the economy; (2) growth (or decline) associated with an increase (or decrease) in the group's participation in the employed labor force; and (3) growth (or decline) associated with the pure shift of the group into or out of the industry. In other words, the shift measure indicates the gains or losses in a given group's penetration of a particular industry, everything else held constant. It is a direct function of the occupational restructuring associated with the reorganization of work. For each group, the shift measure is shown in terms of a turnover, that is, the number of workers shifted around during the ten-year period shown as a percentage of the group's 1980 employment. In addition, the positive and negative shifts are distributed in percentage terms among industries. The overall impact of the shift is illustrated with normalized shares for 1970 and 1980, showing the group's relative standing in an industry vis-à-vis the total labor force. A ratio below 1 means that the group penetration of the industry is lagging; a ratio above 1 indicates that the group is overrepresented.

For example, Table 6.2 shows a turnover measure of 2.6 percent for white women, indicating that 2.6 percent of the 34,806,839 white women were shifted around between 1970 and 1980, ending up in an industry different from that in which they would have been employed had there been no change in the penetration of various sectors of the economy by white women. This shift was due primarily to increased penetration in public administration (explaining 25.8 percent of the positive shift), other goods (+20.9 percent), and FIRE (Finance, Insurance and Real

Estate) and business services (respectively, +14.7 percent and +11.5 percent) matched by a decreased penetration in education (explaining 37.9 percent of the negative shift), manufacturing (−32.1 percent), and health (−28.4 percent).

On the whole, Table 6.2 suggests the following: Shifts were very extensive among black females (turnover of 13.9 percent for the entire group) and youths (8.3 percent turnover) and rather limited among white females (2.6 percent turnover), Hispanic males (3.3 percent), and black males (4.3 percent). The greatest move by black females was out of the consumer-service industries where large numbers once were employed as domestic servants. Their greatest gains were in manufacturing (+29.4 percent); public administration (+18.2 percent); FIRE and TCU (Transportation, Communication and Utilities) (+29.1 percent combined), where they made large gains in clerical positions; and the educational sector (+9.4 percent), where black females made great gains as teachers. Greatest losses for youth were in TCU, FIRE, and business services (51.1 percent of their losses combined), while their greatest gains were in retailing (a staggering 80.6 percent!). These findings are highly consistent with the analysis presented earlier in this chapter.

The patterns of gains and losses among Hispanic females tended to resemble those of black females, with slight differences. In the case of black and Hispanic males, the common finding was that their limited positive shifts were overwhelmingly concentrated in some of the least dynamic and slowest-growing sectors of the economy: manufacturing and TCU for black males (+71.4 percent) and manufacturing and construction for Hispanic males (+92.8 percent). In the case of white women, industry shifts over the decade were very limited (overall turnover of only 2.6 percent).

The second set of data, presented in Table 6.3, shows changes in the normalized shares of major groups of workers in primary occupations in 1966, 1978, and 1981. These data are for large private-sector firms only (100 employees) and are based on EEO–1 reports. The data show progress made by various groups of workers in what has been traditionally the most progressive sector of the economy in terms of EEO enforcement— the large employers.

Some major changes are worth highlighting. The data show white women shifting out of clerical positions and making great gains in professional positions; black and Hispanic women shifting out of service-worker and laborer positions, respectively, and making large gains in clerical positions; black and Hispanic males moving out of laborer positions into operative and craft worker positions. Minority males in general continued to trail considerably in all of the fastest-growing

TABLE 6.2
Industry Shifts of Major Groups of Workers and Distribution of Positive and Negative Shifts Among Industries, 1970–1980

	Employment Distribution All Sex, Race & Age		Youth (16–19 Yrs. Old)				Black Female				Hispanic Female			
	1980 %	1970 %	Normalized Share 1980	1970	Shift (%) +	−	Normalized Share 1980	1970	Shift (%) +	−	Normalized Share 1980	1970	Shift (%) +	−
1. Health	7.4	5.5	0.68	0.93		−21.3	2.35	2.35	+ 0.3		1.42	1.81		−23.6
2. FIRE	6.0	5.0	0.67	0.85		−13.2	1.03	0.70	+15.1		1.23	1.17	+ 3.4	
3. Social	1.8	1.6	0.87	0.70	+ 3.1		2.13	1.32	+10.5		1.48	1.18	+10.7	
4. Bus. Serv.[a]	6.6	5.7	0.72	0.90		−14.7	0.60	0.85		−10.6	0.73	0.83		− 6.6
5. Education	8.6	8.0	0.62	0.75		−13.5	1.59	1.49	+ 9.4		1.14	1.11	+12.4	
6. TCU	7.3	6.8	0.33	0.59		−23.2	0.71	0.44	+14.8		0.52	0.49	+ 6.8	
7. Wholesale	4.3	4.1	0.71	0.68	+ 0.8		0.34	0.32	+ 0.8		0.71	0.81		− 7.3
8. Construction	5.9	6.0	0.71	0.52	+12.9		0.10	0.06	+ 1.4		0.14	0.11	+ 0.8	
9. Public Adm.	5.3	5.5	0.40	0.37	+ 1.9		1.51	1.07	+18.2		0.90	0.73	+16.8	
10. Cons. Serv.[b]	20.3	21.4	2.46	2.11	+80.6		1.06	1.70		−86.1	1.23	1.39		−62.5
11. Other Goods[c]	4.0	4.5	1.06	1.02	+ 0.7		0.20	0.33		− 3.4	0.59	0.56	+ 0.2	
12. Manufacturing	22.4	25.9	0.60	0.64		−14.1	0.78	0.60	+29.4		1.14	0.96	+52.3	
	100.0	100.0			100.0	100.0			100.0	100.0			100.0	100.0
1980 Employment			6,973,441				4,659,177				2,168,649			
Turnover (% 1980 empl.)			8.3%				13.9%				5.7%			

[a] legal, accounting, advertising, and the like
[b] retailing and personal services
[c] agriculture, mining

TABLE 6.2 continued

	White Female			Black Male			Hispanic Male		
	Normalized Share		Shift (%)	Normalized Share		Shift (%)	Normalized Share		Shift (%)
	1980	1970	+ −	1980	1970	+ −	1980	1970	+ −
1. Health	1.74	1.93	−28.4	0.65	0.58	+ 7.7	0.42	0.46	− 3.4
2. FIRE	1.43	1.41	+14.7	0.58	0.53	+ 4.5	0.54	0.61	− 8.3
3. Social	1.45	1.32	+ 8.1	0.84	0.86	− 2.1	0.48	0.61	− 7.4
4. Bus. Serv.[a]	0.92	0.90	+11.5	0.82	0.84	− 4.9	0.98	0.96	+ 7.2
5. Education	1.53	1.70	−37.9	0.68	0.54	+16.4	0.42	0.45	− 6.9
6. TCU	0.56	0.59	− 1.5	1.72	1.45	+38.5	1.12	1.17	−11.3
7. Wholesale	0.67	0.65	+ 4.7	0.96	1.00	− 7.2	1.18	1.25	−11.3
8. Construction	0.21	0.17	+10.8	1.37	1.56	−29.5	1.70	1.47	+34.4
9. Public Adm.	0.88	0.77	+25.8	1.33	1.32	− 1.7	0.87	1.12	−44.0
10. Cons. Serv.[b]	1.30	1.28	+ 3.4	0.72	0.74	−16.7	0.90	0.90	− 2.9
11. Other Goods[c]	0.40	0.27	+20.9	0.88	1.30	−37.8	2.04	1.97	− 4.5
12. Manufacturing	0.72	0.77	−32.1	1.29	1.21	+32.9	1.26	1.10	+58.4
1980 Employment	34,806,839	100.0	100.0	4,674,871	100.0	100.0	3,288,208	100.0	100.0
Turnover (% 1980 empl.)	2.6%			4.3%			3.3%		

Note: The twelve industries are ranked by rate of growth between 1970 and 1980 from the fastest growing (health) to the slowest growing (manufacturing). The industry breakdown used is based on the classification of service industries developed in Thomas M. Stanback, Jr., Peter J. Bearse, Thierry J. Noyelle and Robert A. Karasek, *Services/The New Economy* (Totowa, N.J.: Rowman & Allanheld, 1981). The first two columns show the distribution of all employed among the twelve industries in 1970 and 1980. The positive and negative "shift" is distributed for each group on a percentage basis. The normalized shares of major groups of workers shown for 1970 and 1980 are computed by dividing the share of employment held by each group in each industry by that same group's share of all employment in all industries combined. An index below 1.00 indicates underrepresentation; above 1, overrepresentation. For definition of "shift," see text.

Source: U.S. *Census of Population, Detailed Characteristics of the Labor Force,* 1970 and 1980.

TABLE 6.3
Employment of Major Groups of Workers in EEO-Reporting Firms by Sex, Race, and Occupation: All Industries, 1966, 1978, and 1981

| | EEO Firm Employees Distributed by Occupation | | | Normalized Shares | | | | | |
| | | | | White Male | | | White Female | | |
	1981	1978	1966	1981	1978	1966	1981	1978	1966
Managers and Administrators	11.7	10.8	8.2	1.54	1.56	1.47	0.55	0.48	0.32
Professionals	9.7	8.6	6.6	1.17	1.21	1.38	1.01	0.96	0.46
Technicians	5.7	5.0	4.5	1.10	1.10	1.09	0.98	0.98	0.99
Sales Workers	9.0	8.8	7.1	0.86	0.88	0.98	1.40	1.39	1.30
Clerical Workers	16.3	15.6	16.7	0.27	0.30	0.43	2.07	2.16	2.43
Craft Workers	12.1	12.6	14.2	1.63	1.58	1.46	0.21	0.21	0.20
Operatives	19.1	21.1	25.4	1.06	1.04	1.00	0.72	0.75	0.85
Laborers	7.5	8.5	9.7	0.92	0.89	0.86	0.70	0.74	0.66
Service Workers	9.1	9.0	7.7	0.61	0.60	0.66	1.15	1.21	1.13
	100.0	100.0	100.0						
% of EEO Employed				48.0	50.2	60.6	33.0	31.7	28.0

TABLE 6.3
(Continued)

	Black Male			Black Female			Hispanic Male			Hispanic Female		
	1981	1978	1966	1981	1978	1966	1981	1978	1966	1981	1978	1966
Managers and Administrators	0.47	0.41	0.12	0.27	0.21	0.08	0.50	0.48	0.31	0.27	0.21	0.10
Professionals	0.32	0.30	0.13	0.44	0.40	0.24	0.35	0.39	0.37	0.32	0.32	0.16
Technicians	0.63	0.57	0.26	0.89	0.92	1.03	0.68	0.68	0.53	0.59	0.63	0.56
Sales Workers	0.48	0.43	0.17	0.80	0.77	0.56	0.56	0.52	0.41	1.00	0.89	0.92
Clerical Workers	0.35	0.30	0.16	1.73	1.65	1.05	0.29	0.29	0.31	1.73	1.68	1.39
Craft Workers	1.20	1.10	0.55	0.22	0.21	0.17	1.38	1.32	1.01	0.27	0.32	0.33
Operatives	1.68	1.67	1.46	1.09	1.12	0.98	1.41	1.39	1.30	1.18	1.16	1.15
Laborers	2.08	2.06	3.07	1.16	1.21	1.45	2.47	2.48	2.79	1.73	1.84	1.74
Service Workers	1.65	1.60	2.32	2.20	2.35	3.93	1.47	1.35	1.62	1.59	1.58	1.57
% of EEO Employed	6.0	6.3	5.7	5.5	5.2	2.5	3.4	3.1	1.7	2.2	1.9	0.8

Note: The first three columns of the table show the distribution of all EEO firm employees (all sexes and races combined) by occupation for 1966, 1978, and 1981, respectively. These three columns indicate the changing relative importance of the major occupations in EEO reporting firms in 1966, 1978, and 1981. The normalized shares of major groups of workers shown for 1966, 1978, and 1981 in the remainder of the table are computed by dividing the share of employment held by each group in each occupation by that group's share of all employment in EEO reporting firms (shown on the last line of the table). An index below 1 indicates underrepresentation; an index above 1 indicates overrepresentation.

Source: U.S. Equal Employment Opportunity Commission, *Minorities and Women in Private Industry, EEO-1 Reports* (Washington, D.C.: Government Printing Office, 1966, 1978, and 1981).

white-collar organizations despite some scattered gains. Of all groups, Hispanic males appeared to have been the least mobile.

In all, these data are broadly consistent with several of the tendencies suggested in this and earlier chapters. They suggest that the 1970s were characterized by a good deal of change in terms of access to various employment opportunities by various groups of workers, the reasons being that some sectors shrank (e.g., manufacturing), while others grew (e.g. services) and that employers reorganized their internal employment policies and practices in response to the growing availability of college-educated labor, technological change, and other factors.

These data also suggest that some upward mobility, measured in occupational terms, was achieved by groups historically discriminated against, even though achievements remained uneven. Clearly, also, progress often came through educational credentials rather than through internal job ladders.

Last, these data suggest that, in the aggregate, women fare better than minority men, not simply in entering professional and technical occupations but in progressing further into white-collar occupations where the future of the work world lies. Minority men, especially Hispanic men, failed largely in entering the white-collar world in great numbers, suggesting troubles ahead.

Conclusion:
The Changing Nature of Job Segmentation

The analyses presented throughout this book point strongly to the emergence of new labor markets. The rising importance of service industries, the rise of higher education, the renewed importance of market competition, the coming of age of new information technologies, and yet other factors have had a profound effect on the structure of markets and on the organization of employment systems. Traditional employment attributes are changing, and a new labor market dynamic is emerging.

Under the new dynamic, the role of the firm as the principal locus of upward mobility is weakening, except perhaps for workers in the highest echelons. Increasingly, mobility must be sought through job hopping and additional education. To repeat, what we seem to be witnessing is a transformation of employment characteristics and mobility opportunities such that increasing numbers of workers in a growing number of occupations are now experiencing employment conditions that have long been akin to the traditional professions. This new dynamic, which is taking hold principally among top- and middle-tier jobs, seems to put a much greater premium on the role of educational opportunities and social networks in acceding to new jobs. This process is likely to favor some groups of disadvantaged workers over others (especially, although not exclusively, white women over minority men and women) and, as a result, may shift the nature of handicaps. In addition, the weakening attachment of firms to employees, the relative loss of sheltering from competition which workers attained in the past when many jobs were industry or firm specific, and yet other factors may well explain why, in some areas, we are witnessing both *upskilling* and *downwaging* (National Association of Working Women, 1985). The policy implications of some of these changes are considered in the final chapter.

Are all of the changes identified in this book contributing to a dramatic restructuring of the job segments that had taken shape under industrial dualism? Most likely they are, but it is difficult to be specific, given the materials at hand. Most of the findings of this book pertain to what is happening on the demand side of the labor market. This book does not attempt to identify the dynamics of change on the supply side, except for the very sketchy argument developed in the closing section of this chapter. Paradoxically, however, the analyses presented here suggest that the restructuring of employment systems by firms has been determined, in large part, by changes taking place in the structuring of the labor supply. In other words, the mechanisms that are shaping the supply of labor have become increasingly important in shaping labor demand. During the industrial period, the quantity of available labor was a prime concern of employers in their relationship with the external labor market. Employers would shape labor to their liking by means of the internal labor market structure. In the new service economy, quality of labor becomes a major preoccupation; employers are organizing employment systems around the very notion that external labor pools have become qualitatively stratified.

To the best of my knowledge, thus far there have been very few attempts by labor market economists to understand the new supply-side dynamics (among notable exceptions are Bailey and Waldinger's work [1984] on youth and Bailey's work [forthcoming] on low-wage labor). Short of an extensive understanding of the dynamics of job hopping and employment mobility in the new economy, we will remain highly constrained in our ability to conceptualize further the dynamics of the new labor market dynamics.

7

Policy Implications

From a policy perspective, the materials presented in this book suggest that the new era calls not simply for a fine tuning of existing labor market policies but also for a major revamping of the policy apparatus. To the extent that the new labor markets are still in an early developmental stage, there remains considerable opportunity to shape their contours and dynamics. The task is likely to be formidable, however, since it will probably run against entrenched interests and, in particular, against current, dominant ideological views that often bear little resemblance to the realities described in this manuscript.

In this closing chapter, I discuss four areas: (1) the changing nature of mobility; (2) the changing role of educational institutions and labor market mediating institutions; (3) the implications of labor market transformation for distributional policies; and (4) possible responses by government, trade unions, and employers.

The Changing Nature of Mobility

The changing nature of labor market mobility points to new critical policy areas.

One such critical area is the linkage between employment opportunity and educational credentials. The increasing importance of formal educational credentials, particularly higher educational credentials from junior colleges and up, means that workers who succeed in acquiring such credentials are likely to fare far better than those who do not.

Proponents of dual labor market theory traditionally argued that, while differences in educational credentials had long existed, such differences played a minor role in explaining the dynamics of labor market segmentation. Indeed, to the extent that most workers in the industrial era entered the world of work with roughly similar and typically limited levels of education (four or fewer years of high school), educational attainment could barely explain long-term differences in labor market achievement.

In light of my earlier analyses, two observations must be made. The first observation is that educational achievements and labor market achievements are becoming increasingly intertwined as firms are pressed to externalize more of the training responsibility to higher educational institutions. Hence, to the extent that discrimination occurs in the process by which workers acquire additional increments of training and education, such discrimination becomes an increasingly important determinant of overall labor market discrimination.

From the viewpoint of affirmative action, this poses two new problems. Previously focused on dismantling discrimination within internal labor markets, EEO policies must now pay much greater attention to the importance of the linkage between educational opportunities and employment opportunities. For example, if employers are responsible for creating new educational opportunities through company-sponsored training programs, affirmative action must increasingly focus on the rules by which employees are admitted into such programs. In particular, given the current tendency to shift training to educational institutions such as vocational schools, community colleges, and four-year colleges, we need to understand whether or not the selection criteria instituted by educational institutions are discriminatory. In addition, if the bulk of basic educational preparation is acquired at a worker's own initiative, we must pay much greater attention to the extent to which the current administration's attempts to cut into higher educational support may bear more heavily on some workers rather than on others, and undermine efforts to open access to better jobs for the disadvantaged.

The second observation is that the need for increasing attention to educational discrimination does not mean to imply that if all were given equal access to similar education, labor market discrimination would be eliminated. While one is not going to become a practicing physician without proper credentials, this does not guarantee a workplace free of discrimination. In fact, two recent studies assessing the gains (or lack thereof) of black men in the Washington, D.C., area labor market point to the continuing need to pay attention to other forms of employment discrimination. Both studies found that underemployment of four-year-college-educated males remained greater among black males than among white males. In one study, underemployment was measured by comparing unemployment rates among four-year-college-educated workers (Washington Urban League, 1985) and in the other study by comparing the shares of professionals and managers among four-year-college-educated workers (Grier and Grier, 1985).

In the first study, unemployment was found to be higher among college-educated black males than among white males; in the second, the shares of college-educated men employed as professionals or managers were found to be lower among black men than among white men. While such discrepancies might have been explained partly by a greater mismatch between the demand for certain college skills and the supply of those skills among such groups, such a mismatch remained insufficient to explain fully the discrepancy. Clearly, workplace discrimination remained, a point underscored by the fact that recent employment growth in the Washington, D.C., area has been mostly in the producer service industries (such as legal services, accounting, consulting, and so forth), which by virtue of being relatively new, have never been a principal target of EEO enforcement and in fact have a rather poor EEO record.

Another critical policy area opened up as a result of the shifting nature of mobility and the disappearance of internal labor markets is the extent to which mobility opportunities might have shrunk. At this point in the development of the new labor markets, this would appear to be a problem principally for the lower two tiers of the labor market.

In terms of the middle tier of the labor market, the lack of mobility may in part be the result of deficient labor market information, including a lack of understanding on the part of clerical workers with computer training that their skills are largely transferable to other firms and other industries. In a broader sense, the scope of mobility opportunities for many middle-tier workers may also have a great deal to do with the way in which the paraprofessionalization of their occupations is carried out since the process can either increase the scope of responsibilities or confine it. Two factors are critical.

First, if paraprofessionalization is handled by individual firms as they prepare workers to work on new systems, the degree of universalization of training may be more restricted than if training is developed outside firms by educational institutions whose objective is to teach skills that can transcend the specific needs of specific employers. In this sense, the shift toward the externalization of training may prove beneficial.

Second, upper-tier workers may stand in the way of the paraprofessionalization of middle-tier workers in that the process of paraprofessionalization often implies a new sharing of professional responsibilities that infringes on the traditional domains of the professions. For example, paralegal personnel may be trained to retrieve relevant legal material or to prepare new legal documents but may be forbidden to use these documents in a legal procedure, as is usually the case now. By comparison, paralegals could be trained and allowed to handle simple legal matters such as divorce proceedings or immigration procedures. Similar examples abound in many other occupational interfaces, such as those between nurses and doctors; between information technicians, librarians, and information users; or between robot technicians and engineers. Potentially, however, greater openness of the scope of para-professionalization may ease lateral mobility, while diminishing the gap between the middle and upper tiers of the labor market.

In regard to workers in the lower tier of the labor market, the issue of mobility may be posed in quite different terms depending on the labor market characteristics of the particular group of workers. If these low-skilled jobs are, for example, short-term positions for young workers supporting themselves as they prepare for better jobs at junior or four-year colleges, then they may serve a useful function. By comparison, if they become dead-end jobs for groups of mature workers, it simply says that the emerging labor market has not yet learned how to eliminate this type of work. In this respect, what remains unclear is the extent to which many of these jobs, sooner or later, may be fundamentally transformed by the new technology.

The Changing Role of Educational Institutions and Labor Market Mediating Institutions

All that has been said thus far points to the changing role of educational institutions and, more importantly perhaps, to the need for changing the way educational institutions operate. We are moving into an era in which the traditional separation between working and learning is disappearing, with learning becoming increasingly integrated into a person's work life. Yet, most higher educational institutions remain geared to meeting the needs of an economic world in which formal higher education is seen largely as a once-in-a-lifetime opportunity, preferably in one's younger years.

From a policy research point of view, a great deal of work needs to be done to sort out the implications of the current transformation for higher educational policies and institutions and, even more broadly perhaps, to transform a broad range of labor market mediating institutions.

My analyses point to the fact that the role of the firms as the central labor market mediating institution—as a provider of stable long-term employment relationships, opportunities for upward mobility, or new training—is declining. If that is the case, the issue is which institutions will help workers progress through their careers by way of frequent training or retraining and frequent job changes. Clearly, educational institutions, unemployment compensation, and perhaps even welfare need to play an ever-increasing role in the process of adjustment. Yet, these elements remain the product of a previous era in which the firm was largely responsible for coordinating labor market adjustments. We continue to lay off people with unemployment compensation but make no provision for their retraining. We continue to lag in training for new skills. Much remains to be done to rethink the linkages among many of these institutions.

The Implications of Labor Market Transformation for Earnings and Distributional Policies

The tendency toward a weakening of internal labor markets and the delinking of mobility opportunities from one's place of employment appears to have threatened wage rates and social benefits. Using information on employee benefits presented in a recent publication from the U.S. Department of Labor (1984), Appelbaum argues that there is evidence that: "firms are adjusting to technology and other changes in their environment by reorganizing on a core and rung basis, holding to a minimum the number of workers who can expect to have a future with the company and for whom the company is willing to provide health and life insurance and retirement benefits" (Appelbaum, 1985, p. 5). I stressed earlier in this book that this relative drop in wage rates or benefit levels need not be linked to deskilling, simply to deinstitutionalization of the traditional relationship between employment and benefits. In the short term, the decrease in firm-specific employment made possible in part by the trend toward professionalization and paraprofessionalization weakens the degree of sheltering that workers may have had in the past in bargaining with employers, placing more workers in competition with one another and making it easier for employers to bid wage rates down.

This tendency, as well as the decline in the numbers of relatively well-paid, subordinate primary-worker jobs once associated with employment in manufacturing industries and the recent trend sustaining high levels of unemployment and underemployment, all support the notion that the distribution of earnings, benefits, and income has widened, rather than narrowed in recent years. Given the new structure of labor market mobility, however, these trends militate in favor of renewed emphasis on progressive income tax policies, guaranteed income policies, and the generalization of basic social benefits, such as medical and dental insurance and worker compensation, at the federal level rather than the firm level.

But there are other ways in which the current transformation is failing to solve labor market problems. Following the substantial improvements brought about by the War Against Poverty, poverty rates (measured as the share of people living in households with incomes below 125 percent of the official minimum) began climbing steadily again after 1973, from 12.8 to nearly 19 percent in 1984! The timing of the reversal of the trend underscores the fact that the phenomenon is not simply the result of the current administration's policies—even though budgetary cuts have greatly aggravated the trend—but is a structural phenomenon linked to the economic and labor market transformations that have been in the making for at least a decade or so.

In effect, this points to the resurgence of labor market distress. Daniel Saks (1983; 1985), a former research director of the National Commission for Employment Policy, once identified the following three categories in distressed labor market of the early 1980s: (1) unemployed mature workers, (2) underemployed and underpaid mature workers, and (3) unemployed youth.

According to Saks, unemployed mature workers constitute only a small segment of the distressed population, or *new poor*. Saks found that only 20 to 30 percent of below poverty-line earnings could be attributed in the early 1980s to sudden labor market dislocation (i.e., unemployment). Typically, a large share of the dislocated workers found new employment within a reasonable period of time. In the long run, only a small subset comprising mostly older workers from industries hit particularly hard by structural adjustment, joined the ranks of the new poor. The largest share of the new poor came from the under-employed-underpaid mature workers or unemployed youth.

The relatively large group of underemployed-underpaid mature workers found among the new poor constituted a direct manifestation of the deinstitutionalization of earnings and social benefits associated with the new economy.

The group of unemployed youth, including many high school dropouts, minority youth, and young minority men, pointed vividly to the failure of our primary and secondary school system and to the fact that our society was in the process of creating a class of permanently unemployable or underemployable individuals. There are, of course, still jobs that demand very few skills, but it seems doubtful that there will be a sufficient number of such jobs to go around, given the historical tendency toward some broad upgrading in hiring requirements. In the current context of transformation, a repetition of the late 1960s—when the economy ran full speed, and unemployment rates dropped to a mini-mum—is unlikely. In a manufacturing economy, most people were employable if they were willing to expend physical power. This is no longer true. This is the paradox of the current recovery in which employers are complaining about labor shortages, while 30 percent or higher unemployment rates continue to prevail among some groups of minority men.

Possible Responses

The Role of Government

The closing observation of the previous section points to one area in which government intervention is most needed. Clearly, the cutbacks in federal training and employment programs have left only the most minimal programs intact. By most accounts, programs carried out under the Job Training and Partnership Act (JTPA) reach only a few. Efforts by private organizations to fill the gaping holes address the problems of only a small number of disadvantaged persons and have no potential, at present, to contribute significantly to the relief of the larger class of unemployed and underemployed. In such a context, we, as a society, are leaving many, especially many youngsters, with little income-generating alternatives but petty crime and other illegitimate activities.

A major public sector effort is needed if we are to relieve the existing situation among the unemployed and underemployed poor. Still, because some of the roots of unemployment can be linked to underschooling in an economy which continues to place increasing emphasis on literacy, such effort must be associated with remedial literacy and skill training, short of which the cycle of unemployment and underemployment will never be broken. Of course, this need for public-sector-sponsored employment programs is not exclusive of other areas where I believe government intervention is needed, including the areas of income distribution and social benefits mentioned earlier.

The Role of Unions

The changing nature of labor market mobility is presenting unions with a major challenge. Clearly, the weakening of company-based mobility and the increasing tendency toward occupationally based mobility have made it more difficult than in the past for unions to identify the institutions which are to be targeted. New ways of organizing workers on an occupational basis have to be identified. This point was raised in an AFL-CIO report, *The Changing Situation of Workers and Their Unions* (1985) but needs more extensive logistical consideration. Perhaps unions need to take a close look at what professional associations and organizations have traditionally done (or failed to do) for their members and reassess some of the lessons of craft unionism from the late nineteenth and early twentieth centuries.

Because of the increasing importance of formal educational credentials, unions might want to become directly involved in the whole training-educational process as a means of regaining some control over what is happening in the labor market. Thus far, the most interesting efforts in the work-education nexus have been those deployed by the United Auto Workers (UAW) in the auto industry and the Communication Workers of America (CWA) in telecommunications.

Also, in an era in which work is being so profoundly redefined, unions will only lose if they restrict bargaining efforts to preserving employment structures that are becoming increasingly obsolete. Unions must participate in negotiating and shaping new ways of dividing the entire work process.

The Role of Employers

On the part of employers, the greatest dangers lie in confusing the renewed need for flexibility with indiscriminate cost cutting. The demand for greater flexibility is partly a response to renewed competition, which is itself partly a reflection of a dramatic shortening of the product cycle. This shortened cycle is pressuring firms to move in and out of markets faster than they had been used to traditionally. These transformations, however, are taking place against the background of the introduction of new technologies.

In a broad sense, these new technologies are bringing about an overall upskilling of the labor force. More than ever before, there is a need to invest in the preparation of the labor force. Put another way, the capacity of the economy to expand is increasingly related to the investment it is willing to make in human capital. In this context, flexibility simply means that the locus of that investment is shifting away from the firm toward other institutions, not that the cost of the investment has somehow dissipated. In the end, investment has to be paid out of the surplus of the economy, even though each firm may no longer be able to associate directly the benefits of the human resource investment with its own profit growth. The tendency to see this investment as yet an additional tax burden is great, and the temptation to ask for a reduction in public programs, enormous. Here lies a major paradox which, in my opinion, our society has not yet confronted.

Bibliography

Adler, Paul, "Technology and Us," Working Paper, Stanford: Department of Industrial Engineering, Stanford University, 1985.

Adler, Paul, "Rethinking the Skill Requirements of New Technologies," Working Paper HBS 84–27, Cambridge: Division of Research, Harvard Business School, 1984.

Adler, Paul, and Norman Bowers, "History vs. Segmentation: Segmented Work, Divided Workers, A Review Essay," unpublished, 1983.

AFL-CIO, The Changing Condition of Workers and Their Unions, Washington, D.C.: AFL-CIO, 1985.

American Telephone and Telegraph, 1981 Annual Report.

Appelbaum, Eileen, "Alternative Work Schedules of Women," Working Paper, Philadelphia: Department of Economics, Temple University, 1985.

Appelbaum, Eileen, Technological Change in the Insurance Industry: 1960–90, Research Report, Philadelphia: Department of Economics, Temple University, 1984.

Averitt, Robert T., The Dual Economy: The Dynamics of American Industry Structure, New York: W.W. Norton, 1968.

Bailey, Thomas, Immigrants and Native Workers: Contrasts and Competition. Boulder: Westview Press, 1987.

Bailey, Thomas, and Roger Waldinger, "New York Labor Market: A Skill Mismatch," New York Affairs, Summer 1984.

Baran, Barbara, "The Technological Transformation of White Collar Work: A Case Study of the Insurance Industry," Working Paper, Berkeley: Berkeley Round Table on the International Economy, University of California, 1985.

Bertrand, Olivier, and Thierry J. Noyelle, Gestion des Resources Humaines et Technologies aux Etats Unis, Research Report, Paris: Ministere de l'Education Nationale/CEREQ, 1985.

Bertrand, Olivier, and Thierry J. Noyelle, The Development and Utilization of Human Resources in the Context of Technological Change and Industrial Restructuring: The Case of White Collar Workers, Expert Report, Paris: OECD/CERI, 1984 (OECD/CERI/CD[85]8).

Bluestone, Barry, and Mary Huff Stevenson, "Industrial Transformation and the Evolution of Dual Labor Markets" in Frank Wilkinson, editor, The Dynamics of Labor Market Segmentation, New York: Academic Press, 1981.

Bluestone, Barry, Patricia Hanna, Sarah Kuhn, and Laura Moore, The Retail Revolution, Boston: Auburn House, 1981.

Braverman, Harry, *Labor and Monopoly Capital: The Degradation of Work in the Twentieth Century*, New York: Monthly Review Press, 1974.

Burris, Beverly H., *No Room at the Top*, New York: Praeger Publishers, 1983.

Center on Educational Research and Innovation, *The Development and Utilization of Human Resources in the Context of Technological Change and Industrial Restructuring: A Synthesis of the OECD/CERI Case Studies in the Automobile Industry*, Paris: OECD/CERI, 1984 (OECD/CERI/CD[85]10).

Christopherson, Susan, and Michael Storper, "After Mass Production: Vertical Disintegration, Flexible Specialization, and Agglomeration. The Case of the U.S. Motion Picture Industry," Working Paper, Los Angeles: Urban Planning Program, University of California, 1985.

Doeringer, Peter, and Michael J. Piore, *Internal Labor Markets and Manpower Analysis*, Lexington, Mass.: D.C. Heath/Lexington Books, 1971.

Edwards, Richard C., *Contested Terrain*, New York: Basic Books, 1979.

Edwards, Richard C., Michael Reich, and David M. Gordon, editors, *Labor Market Segmentation*, Lexington, Mass.: Lexington Books, 1973.

Ellis, Joseph, *R. H. Macy & Co.,*, Research Report, New York: Goldman Sachs Investment, April 10, 1978.

Freedman, Marcia K., *Training for Telecommunications Occupations*, Research Report, New York: Center for Advanced Technology in Telecommunications, Polytechnic Institute of New York, 1984.

Gallo, Carmenza, "The Construction Industry in New York City," Working Paper, New York: Conservation of Human Resources, Columbia University, 1983.

Ginzberg, Eli, Thierry J. Noyelle, and Thomas M. Stanback, Jr., *Technology and Employment: Concepts and Clarifications*, Boulder: Westview Press, 1986.

Ginzberg, Eli, and George J. Vojta, "The Service Sector of the U.S. Economy," *Scientific American*, Vol. 244, #3, March 1981.

Gordon, David M., *The Working Poor: Towards a State Agenda*, Washington, D.C.: The Council of State Planning Agencies, 1979.

Gordon, David M., Richard C. Edwards, and Michael Reich, *Segmented Work, Divided Workers*, New York: Oxford University Press, 1982.

Grier, George, and Eunice Grier, *The Washington Labor Force*, Research Report, Washington, D.C.: Greater Washington Research Center, January 1985.

Helbert, Erich A., Eleanor G. May, and Malcolm P. Nair, *Controllership in Department Stores*, Cambridge: Graduate School of Business Administration, Harvard University, 1965.

Hirschhorn, Larry, "Case Study of a Repair Center at Bell Atlantic," Working Paper, Philadelphia: The Wharton Center, The Wharton School, University of Pennsylvania, forthcoming.

Hirschhorn, Larry, "Information Technology and the Office Worker: A Developmental View," Working Paper, Philadelphia: The Wharton Center, The Wharton School, University of Pennsylvania, 1984.

Howard, Robert, "Brave New Work Place," *Working Papers for a New Society*, November/December 1980.

Ichniowski, C. "Have Angels Done More? The Steel Industry Consent Decree," *Industrial and Labor Relations Review*, Vol. 36, #2, January 1983.

Katz, Harry C., *Shifting Gears: Changing Labor Relations in the U.S. Automobile Industry*, Cambridge: The M.I.T. Press, 1985.

Lebhar, Godfrey M., *Chain Stores in America, 1859–1962*, New York: Chain Store Publishing Corporation, 1963.

Moody's Industrial Manuals, New York: Moody's Investors Service, several years.

Moody's Public Utility Manuals, New York: Moody's Investors Service, several years.

National Association of Working Women, *Hidden Victims: Clerical Workers, Automation and the Changing Economy*, Report to the Joyce Foundation, Cleveland: National Association of Working Women, 1985.

Newman, David, "Work and Technology in the Telephone Industry," *Dissent*, Winter 1981.

Northrup, Herbert R., and John A. Larson, *The Impact of the AT&T-EEO Consent Decree*, Labor Relations and Public Policy Series, Vol. 20, Philadelphia: The Wharton School, University of Pennsylvania, 1979.

Noyelle, Thierry J., *New Technologies and Financial Services: A Paradigm for the New Economy*, forthcoming.

Noyelle, Thierry J., *Employment and Career Opportunities of Women and Minorities in a Changing Economy: Preliminary Findings*, Interim Report to the Rockefeller Foundation, New York: Conservation of Human Resources, Columbia University, 1983.

Piore, Michael J., and Charles F. Sabel, *The Second Industrial Divide*, New York: Basic Books, 1984.

Rogers, Everett M., *The High Technology of Silicon Valley*, College Park, Md: The University of Maryland Publications, 1985.

Ryan, Paul, "Segmentation, Duality and the Internal Labor Market," in Wilkinson, *op. cit.*, 1981.

Saks, Daniel H., "A Human Resource Policy for Distressed Workers in a Changing Economy," Working Paper, Nashville: Department of Economics, Vanderbilt University, 1985.

Saks, Daniel H., *Distressed Workers in the Eighties*, Washington, D.C.: National Planning Association, 1983.

Stanback, Thomas M., Jr., *Computerization and the Transformation of Employment, Government, Hospitals, and Universities*, Boulder: Westview Press, 1987.

Stanback, Thomas M., Jr., Peter J. Bearse, Thierry J. Noyelle, and Robert A. Karasek, *Services: The New Economy*, Totowa, N.J.: Rowman & Allanheld, 1981.

U.S. Department of Commerce, Bureau of the Census, *Census of Population, 1980, Detailed Characteristics of the Population*, Washington, D.C.: Government Printing Office, 1970 and 1980.

U.S. Department of Labor, Bureau of Labor Statistics, *Employment and Earnings*, Washington, D.C.: Government Printing Office, monthly, various issues.

U.S. Department of Labor, Bureau of Labor Statistics, *Employee Benefits in Medium and Large Firms*, Bulletin 2213, Washington, D.C.: Government Printing Office, 1984.

U.S. Department of Labor, Bureau of Labor Statistics, *Collective Bargaining in the Telephone Industry*, Report 607, Washington, D.C.: Government Printing Office, June 1980.

U.S. Equal Employment Opportunity Commission, *Minorities and Women in Private Industry*, *EEO–1 Reports*, Washington, D.C.: Government Printing Office, various years.

U.S. Federal Communications Commission, *Statistics of Communications Common Carriers*, annual, various years.

Washington Urban League, *A Profile of Non-Working Blacks Aged 16-64 in Washington D.C.*, *Vol. I: Black Males; Vol. II: Black Females*, Washington, D.C.: Washington Urban League, Inc., 1985.

Wilkinson, Frank, editor, *The Dynamics of Labor Market Segmentation*, New York: Academic Press, 1981.

Newspaper and Magazine Articles

Barron's, "R.H. Macy Boasts Stylish New Image," June 26, 1978.

Business Week, "How Power Will Be Balanced on Saturn's Shop Floor," August 5, 1985.

Business Week, "Hard Lines at AT&T May Force a Strike," March 24, 1980.

Business Week, "The Revolution in the Phone Business," November 6, 1971.

Forbes, untitled article about R.H. Macy & Co, March 15, 1973.

Fortune, "The Service 500," June 10, 1985.

Fortune, "The Distribution Upheaval," series of four articles in April, May, July, and August 1962.

Los Angeles Times, "Ma Bell's New 'Baby' Faces Tough Competition," September 28, 1980.

New York Times, "Companies Turn to Incentives: Incentives Move down the Corporate Ladder," July 19, 1985.

New York Times, "One Life, Ten Jobs," by Ann Crittenden, November 23, 1980.

Wall Street Journal, "Life Insurers Start Offering Policies that Look More Like Investments," February 23, 1983.

About the Author

Thierry J. Noyelle is senior research scholar, Conservation of Human Resources, Columbia University. He is the author of *Business Services in World Markets* (1987) and coauthor of several books, including *Services/The New Economy* (1981), *The Economic Transformation of American Cities* (1984), and *Technology and Employment* (1986).

Index

Employment, 1, 19, 49(n3), 98, 102
AT&T, 50, 53
changes in, 100, 104, 123
data processing, 8, 37
distribution, 42–43(tables)
insurance agencies, 78, 80(table),
83(table), 85–88, 91–95, 96
New York Telephone, 50–51, 57,
61–62, 64–66, 67, 69(table), 71–
75
organizational change, 38–45
patterns, 110–116
prospects, 2, 10–11
quality, 4–5
R. H. Macy & Co., 30–35,
36(table), 38–45
stability, 40–41, 91
See also Equal Employment
Opportunity; Hiring practices;
Job opportunities; Labor market;
Turnover rates;
Underemployment;
Unemployment
Equal Employment Opportunity
(EEO), 41
employment changes, 114–
115(table)
enforcement, 12–15, 111, 120
See also AT&T-EEO-C consent
decree; United States Equal
Employment Opportunity
Commission
ESSs. *See* Electronic switching
systems
Executives, 32(table), 38–39, 48
internal ladders, 64–67
New York Telephone, 57, 62, 64–
67
See also Administrators; Junior
Executives; Managerial positions;
Professional positions; Senior
executives
Exempt personnel, 69, 87. *See also*
Nonexempt employees
External labor markets, 15. *See also*
Internal labor markets;
Recruitment

FCC. *See* Federal Communications
Commission

Federal Communications Commission
(FCC), 52, 58
Finance industry, 4, 37, 95. *See also*
Finance, Insurance and Real
Estate industry
Finance, Insurance and Real Estate
(FIRE) industry, 110–111,
112(table)
Finkelstein, Edward S., 23, 24
FIRE. *See* Finance, Insurance and
Real Estate industry
Fresno, 89–90

General merchandise, 21, 22(table)
Group medical insurance, 82–83

Health industry, 112(table)
Higher education. *See* Education
High technology. *See*
Computerization; Technology
Hiring practices, 49(n3)
insurance companies, 88–89, 91–95
New York Telephone, 68–69
R. H. Macy & Co., 38–39, 41, 44
See also Job opportunities
Hispanics. *See* Minorities
Homogenization, 97–98, 104
Human Resource Development
Division, 70

Income. *See* Earnings
Industrial dualism, 1–2, 5, 15
Industrial period, 1–2
Inflation rates, 78, 79
Information technologies
service economies, 7–10
See also Telecommunications
industry
Insurance industry, 4
changes, 79–81, 95–96
computerization, 83–88
cost control, 80–81
data entry, 105–106
decentralization, 83–88
employment, 78, 80(table),
83(table), 85–88, 91–95, 96
job changes, 110–111
mobility, 12, 89
organizational changes, 81–83, 90
regionalization, 89–90
Internal labor markets, 2–3, 14